I0869395

Documentary Papyri from the Fouad Collection at the Institut Français d'Archéologie Orientale (P.Fouad II 90–100)

Mohamed Gaber Elmaghrabi

Documentary Papyri from the Fouad Collection at the Institut Français d'Archéologie Orientale (P.Fouad II 90–100)

INSTITUT FRANÇAIS D'ARCHÉOLOGIE ORIENTALE

BIBLIOTHÈQUE D'ÉTUDE 186 – 2024

In the same series:

Ali Abdelhalim Ali, Dagmar Budde (eds.), *Mammisis of Egypt: Proceedings of the First International Colloquium, held in Cairo, IFAO, 27–28 March 2019*, 2023.

Mennat-Allah El Dorry (ed.), *Food and Drink in Egypt and Sudan: Selected Studies in Archaeology, Culture, and History*, 2023.

Chloé Ragazzoli, Khaled Hassan, Chiara Salvador (eds.), *Graffiti and Rock Inscriptions from Ancient Egypt: A Companion to Secondary Epigraphy*, 2023.

Paweł Lech Polkowski (ed.), *Stone Canvas: Towards a Better Integration of 'Rock Art' and 'Graffiti' Studies in Egypt and Sudan*, 2023.

Marie-Françoise Boussac, Sylvain Dhennin, Bérangère Redon, Claire Somaglino, Gaëlle Tallet (eds.), *Frontières et marges occidentales de l'Égypte de l'Antiquité au Moyen Âge. Actes du colloque international, Le Caire, 2-3 décembre 2017*, 2023.

Sibylle Emerit, Sylvain Perrot, Alexandre Vincent (eds.), *De la cacophonie à la musique. La perception du son dans les sociétés antiques*, 2022.

Audrey Eller, *Nomes et toparchies en Égypte gréco-romaine. Réalités administratives et géographie religieuse d'Éléphantine à Memphis*, 2022.

Philippe Collombert, Laurent Coulon, Ivan Guermeur, Christophe Thiers (eds.), *Questionner le sphinx. Mélanges offerts à Christiane Zivie-Coche*, 2021.

Hourig Sourouzian, *Recherches sur la statuaire royale de la XIXe dynastie*, 2020.

Thomas Faucher (ed.), *Money Rules! The Monetary Economy of Egypt, from Persians until the Beginning of Islam*, 2020.

© INSTITUT FRANÇAIS D'ARCHÉOLOGIE ORIENTALE, LE CAIRE, 2024

ISBN 978-2-7247-1014-4 ISSN 0259-3823

Mise en page : Christine Mina
Couverture : Ismaïl Seddiq

DANGER
LE PHOTOCOPILLAGE TUE LE LIVRE

Tous droits de traduction, d'adaptation et de reproduction par tous procédés, réservés pour tous pays. Toute reproduction ou représentation intégrale ou partielle, par quelque procédé que ce soit, des pages publiées dans le présent ouvrage, faite sans l'autorisation de l'éditeur, est illicite et constitue une contrefaçon. Seules sont autorisées, d'une part, les reproductions strictement réservées à l'usage privé du copiste et non destinées à une utilisation collective et, d'autre part, les courtes citations justifiées par le caractère scientifique ou d'information de l'œuvre dans laquelle elles sont incorporées (art. L. 122-4, L. 122-5 et L. 335-2 du code de la propriété intellectuelle).

Table of Contents

I dedicate this work as a tribute to my late tutor and mentor Mostafa Elabbadi and as a gratitude to Cornelia Römer.

Acknowledgement

THE PROJECT to publish some of the Fouad Papyri deposited at the Institut Français d'Archéologie Orientale (IFAO) was initiated in 2013, most heartily supported by Sylvie Denoix, then the Director of Studies at the IFAO. At that time, I was engaged in cataloguing this collection at the IFAO's Archives, then headed by Nadine Cherpion.

This project has continued to receive support from the successive Directors of Studies at the IFAO, Nicolas Michel, Frédéric Abécassis, and Abbès Zouache.

A great part of the work was done during a generous "Research in Paris" Senior-Researcher Scholarship granted by the City of Paris for six months in 2015. I am also thankful to Alexandria University for a sabbatical leave during this period.

I benefitted from discussions with Graham Claytor, Dieter Hagedorn, and Robert Daniel, who offered several very helpful suggestions. Thanks also go to Markus Resel for reviewing the indexes.

Above all, I wish to thank Hélène Cuvigny for reading and reviewing the first draft of this manuscript. Any flaws, deficiencies or errors in this book are mine alone.

Mohamed G. Elmaghrabi
Alexandria University
March 2023, Alexandria

Abbreviations

Journal abbreviations follow B. Mathieu, *Abréviations des périodiques et collections en usage à l'Institut français d'archéologie orientale*, 7th ed., Cairo, 2019.

Papyrological editions and congress proceedings follow the abbreviations in J. F. Oates, W. H. Willis et al., *Checklist of Editions of Greek, Latin, Demotic, and Coptic Papyri, Ostraca, and Tablets*.

All dates of cited documents follow in most cases those found in the *Heidelberger Gesamtverzeichnis* (HGV).

Citations of Trismegistos (Deapauw and Geldof 2014) follow the recommendations laid out at http://www.trismegistos.org/about_how_to_cite.php; e.g., (TM Per 136397) = http://www.trismegistos.org/person/136397.

Note on Editorial Conventions

The transcription of the papyri and of all other papyri cited follows the Leiden convention of the set of signs with their customary meanings:

→	Text written along the fibers.
↓	Text written across the fibers.
[ ]	Lacuna.
<αβγδ>	Mistaken omission by the scribe.
[[αβγδ]]	Letters canceled by the scribe.
{αβγδ}	Editorial deletion.
\`αβγδ ´	Scribal insertions above the line of writing.
α̣β̣γ̣δ̣	Badly damaged or uncertainly read letters.
. . . . .	Illegible letters or, in a lacuna, estimated number of letters lost.
(*m.* 2, 3 etc.)	Change in hand
– – – – – –	The papyrus breaks off.

Introduction

In the present volume are edited eleven documentary papyri (one duplicate) from early Roman Egypt. They range in date from 20 CE to 212 CE, but most are from the second century CE. Beside these eleven papyri, a brief description is also given to other two papyri from the collection, inv. 228 and 255 (see **93**, introd.), with a transcription of the latter (see below, p. 4, n. 12).

As indicated in the introduction to *P.Fouad*,[1] most of the papyri published in that volume were purchased in 1930 by the king Fouad I of Egypt and donated to the Société royale égyptienne de Papyrologie (later Société Fouad I de Papyrologie). They were probably bought from Maurice Nahman, from whom the king had purchased in the winter of that very year an inscribed polyhedron.[2]

In the following years, the Société purchased more papyri which were also included in the volume. As the volume was published in 1939, one can only be sure that its 89 papyri were acquired in the period between 1930 and 1939. The highest inventory number in *P.Fouad* is 207 = publication no. 87. It belongs to a coherent group of papyri, *P.Fouad* 86–89, from the monastery of Aphrodito.

These four papyri were a later (single?) purchase by the Société from M. Nahman and were inventoried in a sequence (204–207). They were bought before inv. 208, which was purchased from G. Loukianoff in late 1938, and before the acquisition of inv. 209, the Latin tablet donated by L. Keimer in November 1938. Therefore, we can safely consider that papyri with inventory numbers from 1 to 209 constitute a first phase of the collection, i.e. papyri acquired prior to the publication of *P.Fouad*, and prior to the date, June 1939, when the published papyri were deposited in the Egyptian Museum. A note that may indicate this is written in the Inventory Book of the Société by Octave Guéraud before inventory number 210. All papyri with higher inventory numbers must be later additions. The unpublished papyri were deposited at the IFAO in November 1961 and have been there since then.

1. = *Les Papyrus Fouad I*, ed. Bataille, A. Guéraud, O., Jouguet, P., Lewis, N., Marrou, H.-I., Scherer, J., and Waddell, W. G., Cairo, 1939, Publ. Soc. Fouad 3.
2. It was published by Perdrizet, 1931.

The Inventory Book of the Société contains, in addition to the aforementioned 209 numbers, another 139, making a total of 348 inventory numbers. Presumably the higher the number, the later the piece was acquired. Numbers higher than 209 naturally constitute a second phase of the collection that lasted until at least 1948, when inv. 277 was purchased from Albert Eid. The Inventory Book of the Société provides information about the acquisition of only a few of these papyri. It points to a slow process of acquisition, either through sporadic purchases or donations of a single papyrus or small groups of papyri. This is the case for inv. 258–267, for which we have the following information:

inv. 258–262	donated to the Société by King Farouk I on 14 June 1941
inv. 263–265	purchased from Nahman in 1942
inv. 266	purchased from Tano on 3 April 1943[3]
inv. 267	purchased from Nahman in 1944

From inv. 268 onwards, only the numbers are listed without any further details about when or from whom the pieces were acquired. It is, however, indicated that inv. 259–262 were moved to the Egyptian Museum after 1948 without being published, and that inv. 260–262 were edited by J. Schwartz in *P.Coll.Youtie* 25, 27 and 29 respectively. It may be noted that in the Inventory Book of the Societé a different hand is responsible for inv. numbers 281–348. Whether this relates to a new phase in the acquisition of papyri is an open question.

THE ORIGIN OF THE COLLECTION

Since all the papyri published in the present volume entered the collection, like all other pieces that compose it, as the result of a purchase or a donation, geographical provenances are not indicated in the Inventory Book of the Societé. Information pertaining to provenance is in general sparse. In the introduction to *P.Fouad* 86–89 the editor states that, according to Nahman, these four papyri were acquired from an inhabitant of Asyut, who in turn confirmed to him that they have been found in the neighborhood of this city, i.e. ancient Lykopolis. The editor, however, found this testimony hard to believe.[4] Nevertheless, when the published papyri (either those in *P.Fouad* or later publications as well as the present volume) are arranged according to their inventory numbers, the collection seems to have grown by certain definable phases.

All the published papyri of the first phase—except for the aforementioned inv. 204–209, which seem to be a very late addition to this group—when information about the origin can be gained from the text, originate from either the Arsinoite or Oxyrhynchite nomes. Inv. 131 (= *SB* VI 9262) from the Herakleopolite is not a matter of concern here, it could well have been an Arsinoite or

3. Members of the Tano family were active in Cairo from 1870 to 1977, in the 1940s this Tano should be Phocion Jean Tano [Phokion Ioannis], see Hagen, Ryholt 2016, pp. 265-267.
4. Cf. also Gascou 1978, pp. 157 ff.

Oxyrhynchite find like many other Herakleoplite papyri.[5] Others are still of unknown origin, but in some of these cases, an origin of either the Arsinoite or the Oxyrhynchite is possible. This, for example, is the case for the papyri that belong to the dossier of the family of Zeuxis, (inv. 8, 9, 13, 20, 22, 62, 88, 126 (= **95**), and 128).[6] Only inv. 99 (= *P.Horak* 17) was hypothetically attributed to the Hermopolite nome by its editor on the basis of the reading of λαχαν( ) σε Ερμ( ) in line 8 of the verso, but this has been corrected to λαχανοσπερμ( ).[7] The curious Σομολω in line 9, then, is probably not a place name in the Hermopolite, as the editor suggested, but probably personal name, i.e. the indirect object of ἔδωκα. Although the papyri acquired in the first phase seem to have had various Arsinoite and Oxyrhynchite origins, this is not betrayed by the inventory numbers, which seem to have been assigned to the entire group *en masse*.

No general rule can be applied to the inventory numbers 210 to 226, since most of the published papyri in this range are literary. In 1942 J. Scherer published inv. 211 (= *SB* VI 9016) indicating that it was purchased in April 1941 for the Société from Nahman. Scherer states that it belongs to a group of papyri from the same purchase that originate from Koptos.[8] Scherer perhaps meant the Homeric papyri (inv. 210, 212R°, 213V° and 216V°) that were later published by J. Schwartz, who gives no indication of their origin.[9] In 1951–52, M.-T. Lenger published two papyri from this range, inv. 219 and 222. The first (= *SB* VI 9123) has no reference to provenance, but it is correctly assigned by the editor to the Arsinoite;[10] while inv. 222 is a literary fragment of Aeschines oration against Timarchus to which no provenance is given.[11] Inv. 226 may represent a single purchase; it comprises five pieces of parchment published by J.-L. Fournet as *P.Pintaudi* 59–64 in 2012 with no indication of their origin.

Nevertheless, thirty papyri with inventory numbers 228 to 257 deserve special consideration. According to the Inventory Book of the Société, these papyri were acquired in 1941 sometime between April (when inv. 211 was purchased, see *supra*) and the 14 June 1941 (when inv. 258–262 were dedicated to the Société by King Farouk, see *supra*). When there is information about the origin of any of these papyri, the majority originate from the Lykopolite. This applies to 233 (=*SB* VI 9310) and 236 (=*SB* XVI 12505), both first published by Z. Aly; to 252 A and 256 (= nos. **97–98** in the current volume); and to inv. 255. This last mentioned text is a fragment of what seems to be a draft for an application of lease (or a writing exercise based on such a text)

5. Falivene (1998, p. 34) attributes this document, among other Herakleopolite documents from late Byzantine and early Arabic period, to the first and the second Fayum finds. She, however, does not exclude an Oxyrhynchite provenance for these papyri.
6. For Tebtynis as the provenance of these papyri see van Minnen 1993, p. 118; Elmaghrabi 2020, p. 24.
7. Hagedorn 2004, p. 161.
8. Scherer 1942.
9. Schwartz 1946.
10. Lenger 1951. The papyrus is dated in the second half of the second century BCE and attributed to the Arsinoite because it mentions a *komogrammateus*, named Petearpochrates, who is attested as a *komogrammateus* of Philadelphia in *BGU* VI 1256 in 136 BCE.
11. Lenger 1950-1951.

addressed to a (...) Maximos *strategos* of the Lykopolite and the Hypselite nomes by a man from Lykopolis.[12]

There are two (perhaps seeming) exceptions in the group. The first is 247 (= *SB* VI 9144; cf. *BL* VIII 340). It was first attributed by its editor to Aphrodito since it mentions a pagarch, Flavius Iohannes, who wrote the letter to the people of the Monastery of Apa Apollo. Both the date (589 CE) and the identification of the pagarch had been rejected by J. Gascou,[13] and Fl. Iohannes was later identified with the Hermopolite pagarch with the same name in *P.Lond.* V 1753 (VI-VII).[14] There is nothing in the text that helps to identify the locality of the monastery, but it could be connected with a Lykopolite monastery of Apa Apollo, perhaps the one at Deir el-Bala'izah (TM Geo 3025).

The second exception is an unpublished declaration of death (inv. 249). Since it mentions the *amphodon* Phremei, so far only attested for the capital of the Arsinoite nome, it doubtless pertains to a death that occurred there. But since inv. 249 appears to be the only exception to the Lykopolite provenance of Fouad inv. numbers 228 to 257, it is possible that the papyrus was perhaps brought there by relatives of the deceased. Of course, it remains possible either that inv. 249 was also found in the Fayum and was sold together with the otherwise Lykopolite group or that it was a separate acquisition and inadvertently inventoried with the Lykopolite group.

In view of the above, one may suggest that Lykopolis or its environs is a probable provenance for some of the already published papyri within this range, in any case those that contain no indication to the contrary. This applies to the two private letters published by the late Z. Aly in 1971, namely inv. 253 and 254 (= *SB* XVIII 13864 and XII 10876 respectively). It is noteworthy that these two papyri as well as the aforementioned inv. 236 (= *SB* XVI 12505) became part of Aly's "private" collection (now housed at the Bibliotheca Alexandrina), which includes at least one other papyrus with a definite connection to the Lykopolite and another to the Hypselite, which was later separated from the Lykopolite.[15]

Within the same range of inventory numbers some literary papyri had already been published; these are four Homeric papyri (inv. 230, 242, 244 and the opisthograph 245),[16] a fragment of Aeolic verse (inv. 239),[17] another fragment from Demosthenes' oration against Dionysodoros (inv. 234),[18] and a fragment of a *hypothesis* to Euripides' *Medea* (inv. 248).[19]

12. Inv. 255 is a lease for a single year, the 14th year of Marcus Aurelius (173–174 CE). I offer here a transcription of its twelve preserved lines: [̣ ̣ ̣ ̣ ̣ ̣ Μα]ξίμῳ στρα(τηγῷ) | [Λυκ]οπολ(ίτου) καὶ Ὑψηλ(ίτου). | [παρὰ] ̣ ̣ ̣ ου Διοσκόρου | [τοῦ κ]αὶ Ἡρακλήους τῶν ἀπὸ | [Λύκ]ων πόλ[εως] βούλομαι̣ | [μι]σθώσασθαι πρὸς μόνον | τὸ ἐνεστὸς ιδ (ἔτος) Αὐρηλίου | Ἀντωνίνου Καίσαρος τοῦ κυρ[ίο]υ | (*m.* 2) πρὸς μόνον τὸ ἐν[ε]σ̣(τὸς) ιδ (ἔτος) | Αὐρηλίου Ἀντωνίνο̣υ̣ Κ̣[αίσ]αρος | τοῦ κυρ[ίο]υ *spatium* | (*m.* 3) ἡμῶν πάντων.

13. Gascou 1981, p. 220, n. 1.

14. See Kruit 1994, p. 72. Cf. also Fournet 2000, p. 246, n. 30 where the date is paleographically pushed to VII-VIII CE.

15. Currently these two papyri are being prepared by me for publication, the whole collection is registered under one inventory number 1676.

16. Schwartz 1946.

17. Lobel, Page 1952.

18. Papathomopoulos 1961.

19. Papathomopoulos 1964.

The papyri published in the present volume reflect the same disposition. The nos. **90**, **91**, **92**, **95**, **96** and **99** are all from the first phase of acquisitions (i.e. before 1939) and stem from the Arsinoite with the exception of **90** and **92**, which are from Oxyrhynchos. On the other hand, **93**, **97**, **98** and **100** (?) belong to the range of papyri that are from Lykopolis (i.e. acquired sometimes between April 1941 and 14 June 1941). Only **94** (from the Arsinoite) belongs to the latest phase, being acquired after 1948.

Texts 90–100

90. Registration of an Apprentice, with Appending Oath?

P.Fouad inv. 89 (a)	(fr. 1) w 8.5 × h 13 cm	15.10.20 CE
	(fr. 2) w 4 × h 7.7 cm	20? CE

Oxyrhynchos

Two mutilated fragments, with no apparent physical join, though they possibly are from the same sheet. The bodies of the text of both fragments are written by slow writers, but the hands are not identical. The handwriting in the first fragment is a slow semi-uncial with almost no ligatures, with alpha written in three strokes. Curiously, the *hypographe* is more fluent than the hand of the text itself.

The two fragments reflect the process of apprenticeship in Roman Egypt. After the apprentice contract was drawn up, the apprentice would be registered through the authorities for the purpose of compiling a list of apprentices who would be liable to the trade taxes.[1] Only five such registrations have been published so far. Four of them concern weaving,[2] while one deals with copper forging (χαλκοτυπική).[3] All these texts originate from the city of Oxyrhynchos, which is also the case with our text. The five hitherto published registrations date to the middle or the second half of the first century. The present document, from the seventh year of Tiberius (20 CE), is the earliest apprentice registration known so far.

In the first fragment, Pasion son of Zoilos records the apprenticeship of Zoilos to Apollonios son of Sarapion(?), the master weaver (*didaskalos*). The son Zoilos, being named after the declarant's father, is most probably Pasion's eldest son.

This first fragment is broken at the top and the left margins, but it is partially complete on the right side. Some lines are mutilated but can be securely read or supplemented. The missing upper portion should have included the name of the official(s), to whom the registration was

1. For the apprentice system see Bergamasco 1995; Forselv 1998 ; Perdicoyianni-Paleologou 1999.
2. *P.Mich.* III 170 (49 CE), 171 (58 CE), 172 (62 CE); *SB* XXIV 16186 (70 CE) with two new editions in Reiter 2002, and Bergamasco 2004, pp. 31–35.
3. *PSI* VIII 871 (with *BL* 3.225 and 8.402) (66 CE).

submitted. Of the four published registrations of weavers, the earliest, *P.Mich.* III 170 (49 CE), was addressed to the *topogrammateus* and the *komogrammateus*. The three other registrations were addressed to the farmer of the weavers' tax (ἐκλήμπτωρ γερδίων / γερδιακοῦ). Only *PSI* VIII 871 was a copy (ἀντίγραφον) addressed to the *basilikos grammateus*. It is fairly likely that **90**, like *P.Mich.* III 170, was addressed to both the *topogrammateus* and the *komogrammateus*. The same two officials are responsible for such matters in the same year in *P.Oxy.* II 252 = *W.Chr.* 215 (19–20 CE), which is a notification of a runaway weaver.

The form of the present registration does not follow exactly that of the others. Lines 8–14 have a variant formulation that contains elements found only in petitions (see comm.). Since **90** is the earliest example of such text, its divergence may reflect an early stage in the development of the apprentice registration process.

The other fragment, which bears the same inventory number, and which belongs to the same process, contains an oath sworn by a declarant. This oath was penned in a hand that is different from the one in the registration and from the hand of the declarant who subscribed. There is no apparent physical join between the two fragments, but it is clear that they belonged to the same sheet. It is also difficult to establish the connection between the two fragments, especially since no oath was ever included in other apprentice registrations. The editor of *P.Mich.* III (p. 170) had noticed the absence of oath from these registrations as opposed to the notices of removal of those who had fled or died from the rolls to terminate their liability to taxation; he speculates that the absence of oath can be understood as needless in a declaration of liability. In the absence of parallel documents, two scenarios can be imagined. First, if the two fragments are from a single declaration, then the oath was awkwardly appended after the subscription, as in *P.Oxy.* II 253 (Notice of Removal; Oxyrhynchos, 19 CE) and *C.Pap.Gr.* II 5b = *SB* XIV 11587 (Philadelphia, 47 CE), where the oath was appended under the signatures. One may also speculate that the authorities noted the lack of oath and demanded the declarant to supply one, either appending it in the space below or on a new sheet of papyrus, spelling out the information in the registration in short form. The second scenario is that we are dealing with two different registrations, the first containing an oath, the other not; this would explain the absence of oaths in the apprentice registrations of a later date. On the other hand, the information provided within the oath (fr. (2), 7–9 with comm.) fits a contract rather than a registration; do we have here a contract containing an oath sworn by the tutor?

Fr. (1)

\- - - - - - - - - - - - - - - - - -

→ [. . . . .] ̣παρ[. . . . . .]
[ὥστε μαθεῖν τὴ]ν γερδιακὴν̣
[τέχνην ἀπὸ] τοῦ ἐνεστῶ-
[τος ἑβδόμου ἔ]τους Τιβερίο̣[υ]
[Καίσαρος Σ]ε̣β̣[αστο]ῦ παρὰ δ[ι-]
[δασκάλ]ῳ̣ Ἀπο[λλ]ωνίῳ̣ Σαρα-
[πίωνος] ῥ̣ύ̣μ̣ης [Ὀ]ννώφριος,
[προ]ῆ̣γμαι τὸ ὑπόμν[η]μ̣α̣

[ἐπι]δοῦναι, καὶ ἀξιῶ ἀνα-
[γρά]ψασθαι τὸν Ζωίλον ——
[ἐν] τ̣ῆ̣ τάξι τῶν μ̣αθητῶν
[το]ῦ̣ αὐτοῦ ἔτους ὡς ἐ̣π̣ὶ̣ τῶν
ὁμοίων πρὸς τὸ ἀσ̣υ̣[κ]ο̣φ[άν-]
[τ]η̣τόμ μ' εἶναι.

(*m.* 2) Π̣α̣σ̣ίων Ζωίλου ἐπιδέδωκα
τ̣ὸ̣ ὑπόμνημα.
(ἔτους) ζ Τιβερίου Καίσαρος Σεβαστοῦ,
Φαῶφι ιη̅.

- -

11 l. τάξει || **14** l. [τ]η̣τόν

[90 fr. 1]

TRANSLATION

[To NN and NN the…, from Pasion son of Zoilos. Since I wish to apprentice my son, Zoilos, of the Upper Parembole (?)] that he may learn the weavers trade, from the present seventh year of Tiberius Caesar Augustus, to the master weaver Apollonios son of Sarapion (?) of the quarter of Onnophris, I have been moved to submit an application, and I request to register Zoilos in the list of the apprentices of the same year as in similar cases so that I not be subject to false accusations.

I, Pasion son of Zoilos, have submitted the application.

Year 7 of Tiberius Caesar Augustus. Phaophi 18.

COMMENTARY

1.] ̣ παρ[̣ ̣ ̣ ̣ ̣ ̣]: we expect here a description of the apprentice and his relation to the declarant followed by the quarter in which the apprentice is registered as in the case of the registration *PSI* VIII 871, 10–11, with *BL* 8.402, (Oxyrhynchos, 66 CE): ἀναγρα(φόμενον) ἐ̣πὶ τῆς αὐτῆς λαύρας. Thus, παρ is most likely part of a place name, most probably Παρ[εμβολῆς]. Three such localities are attested in Oxyrhynchos. The two that are most frequently attested in the 1st century are Ἱππέων Παρεμβολή and Λυκίων Παρεμβολή. However, the ambiguous trace of ink at the left edge does not resemble part of *nu*, but rather a rounded letter, perhaps *omega*, making the less well-attested Ἄν]ω̣ Παρ[εμβολῆς], "the Upper Camp", a plausible restoration. For these localities, see Daris 2000, pp. 211–221, s.v.

3. [τέχνην ἀπό]: the number of letters here is two or three letters less than expected, but this exact sequence is attested in *P.Mich.* III 170, 6–8 (Oxyrhynchos, 49 CE) and 171, 10–12 (Oxyrhynchos, 58 CE).

7. ῥ̣ύ̣μ̣ης [Ὀ]ννώφριος: after supplementing the patronymic running from the previous line, there is not enough space to read λαύρας here. The street of Onnophris, after which a district was named, is rarely attested, see Krüger 1990, p. 85; Daris 2000, p. 214. For the definition of ῥύμη as synonymous with ἄγυια, see Lolos 2005, p.164.

8–9. [προ]ῆγμαι τὸ ὑπόμνημα | [ἐπι]δοῦναι: this expression is absent from the other registrations, but, with variations, it is mainly used in petitions, the exact phrase being attested in *P.Oxy.* II 283, 16–17 (Memphis, 45 CE) and *PSI* IX 1067 = *Sel.Pap.* II 303, 13–14 (Antinopolis, 236 CE); cf. also *BGU* VIII 1825, 18–19 (Herakleopolite, I BCE) and 1859, 10–12 (Herakleopolite, 64–44 BCE): προῆγμαι τὴν τοῦ ὑπομνήματος ἐπίδοσιν ποιήσασθαι. For the use of προάγομαι + inf., see Döllstädt 1943, p. 30.

9–11. καὶ ἀξιῶ ἀνα|[γρά]ψασθαι τὸν Ζωίλον | [ἐν] τ̣ῇ τάξι τῶν μ̣αθητῶν: cf. *P.Mich.* III 170, 12–14 (Oxyrhynchos, 49 CE): διὸ ἀξιῶ ἀναγράψεσθ[α]ι τὸν υἱὸν ἐν τοῖς τοῦ αὐτοῦ ἔτους μαθηταῖς ὡς καθήκει; 171, 16–19 (Oxyrhynchos, 58 CE): διὸ ἀξιῶ ἀναγράψασθαι τὸν Ἀμοιτᾶν ἐν τοῖς τοῦ αὐτοῦ ἔτους μαθηταῖς ὡς καθήκει; 172, 14–16 (Oxyrhynchos, 62 CE): διὸ ἀξιῶι (l. ἀξιῶ) ἀναγραφῆναι_τὸν υἱὸν ἐν τῇ τῶν μαθητῶν τάξι (l. τάξει) ὅς (l. ὡς) καθήκει.

PSI VIII 871, 15–16 (Oxyrhynchos, 66 CE): ἀξιῶ ἀναγραφῆναι τοῦτον ἐν τῆι τῶν ὁμοίων τάξει, ὡς καθήκ(ει); *SB* XXIV 16186, 15–18 (Oxyrhynchos, 70 CE): διὸ ἀξιῶι (l. ἀξιῶ) ἀναγραφῆναι τ̣ὸ̣ν̣ υἱὸν ἐν τῇ τῶν μ̣α̣θ[ητῶ]ν̣ τάξει ὡς καθήκ̣ε̣ι̣. ε̣ὐ̣τύχ̣(ει). The construction depends on a participle lost at the beginning of the registration (i.e. βουλόμενος) which is attested in three out of the five published registrations: *P.Mich.* III 170, 4–5; 171, 5–6; *PSI* VIII 871, 6. διό which is used to introduce this clause in *P.Mich.* III 170, 12 and 171, 16 has no place here, nor is it used in *PSI* VIII 871.

12–13. ὡ[ς] ἐ̣π[ὶ τῶν] [ὁμ]οίων: this expression is only used once in the apprentice registration *SB* XXIV 16186, 9–13, in connection with the tax rate paid for the apprentice: ἐπὶ τῷ̣ τάξασθαι ὑπὲρ μὲν τοῦ ἐνε[σ]τ̣ῶτος ἔτους ἀργ(υρίου) (δραχμὰς) ὀκτώι (l. ὀκτώ), ἀπὸ δὲ τ̣ο̣ῦ ἰσιόντος (l. εἰσιόντος) ἔτους τὸ καθῆκον [τέλεσ]μα ὡς ἐπὶ τῶν ὁμοίων: "on condition that I pay eight drachmas for the current year, and starting from the next year the required tax paid by persons of the same category." As there is no mention of the tax here, the expression may have been superfluously copied from the notifications of deaths where we find this expression in the same order.

13–14. πρὸς τὸ ἀσ̣υ̣[κ]ο̣φ[άν|τ]η̣τόμ μ' εἶναι: in registrations, this expression is attested only in *P.Monts.Roca.* IV 68, 8–10 (notification of Death, I–II CE): πρ̣(ὸς) [τὸ ἀ]σικοφάντητόν (l. [ἀ]συκοφάντητόν) μ[ε] [εἶ]ναι.

17–18. (ἔτους) ζ Τιβερίου Καίσαρος Σεβαστοῦ | Φαῶφι ιη̣.: the date was probably followed by the signature of the addressed official, as in *P.Mich.* III 172. The opposite order occurs in *P.Mich.* III 170 and 171: first the signature, then the date.

Fr. (2)

\- -

→ [. . .] . . . . [
[αὐ]τ̣ὸν τὴν γερ̣δ[ιακὴν τέχνην]
[ἀπὸ] τ̣ο̣ῦ̣ ἐ̣νεστῶτ[ος ἑβδόμου ἔτους]
[Τιβε]ρίου Καίσαρ̣[ος Σεβαστοῦ]
[. . . . .] . . . . [. . . . .]
. . . . . . ε . . . . . [. . . . . τὸν]
ἐ̣γδεδομένον [υἱὸν (?) δεδιδαγ-]
μένον τὴν τέχ[νην πᾶσαν ἐντελ-]
ῶ̣ς̣. εὐορκοῦν[τι μέν μοι εὖ]
[εἴ]η̣, ἐπιορκοῦντι̣ δ̣ὲ̣ [τὰ ἐναντία.]
spatium
[(ἔτους) ζ?] Τ̣ιβερίου Καί[σαρος Σεβαστοῦ],
\- -

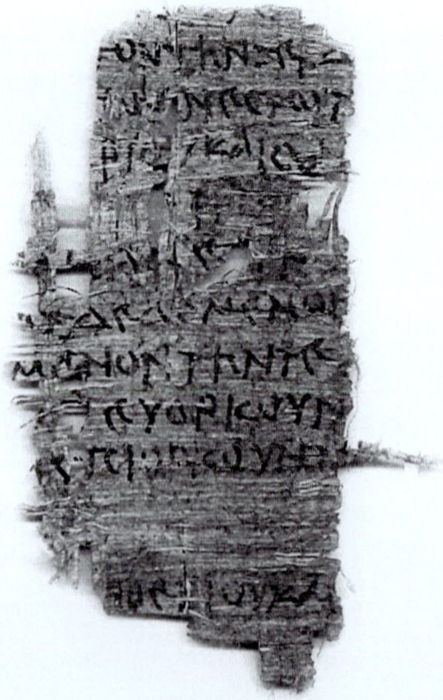

[90 fr. 2]

TRANSLATION

… to teach] him the weaver's trade from the current [seventh year?] of Tiberius Caesar Augustus… the apprenticed having been taught the entire trade in full. If I observe the oath, may it be well with me, but if I swear falsely, the reverse.

[Year 7?] of Tiberius Caesar Augustus. [Month and day]…

COMMENTARY

6–9. . . . . τὸν] | ἐ̣γδεδομένον [υἱὸν (?) δεδιδαγ-]||μένον τὴν τέχ[νην πᾶσαν ἐντελ-]||ῶ̣ς̣: this may reflect a stipulation defined in the original apprentice contract, as e.g. in *SB* XVIII 13305, 23–28 (Karanis, 271 CE): [τ]οῦ χρόνου πληρωθέντος καὶ παραμινάσης τῆς παιδὸς ἀμέμπτως, παραδωσιν (l. παραδώσει) αὐτὴν ἡ δεσκαλος (l. διδάσκαλος) μεμαθηκυῖαν τὴν τέχνην ἐντελῶς καθ' ὁμοιότητα τῶν ὁμηλίκων αὐτῆς. For the significance of the verb ἐκδίδοσθαι in the apprentice contracts see Herrmann 1957–58, pp. 119–39, esp. pp. 134–137. For the use of δεδιδαγμένον in the same context see *SPP* XXII 40, 22–24 (Soknopaiou Nesos, 150 CE): κ[αὶ] μετὰ τὸν χρόνον παραστήσατω τὴ̣ν [παιδίσ]κ̣ην δεδ[ιδ]αγμένην τὴν τέχνην καθά[περ] α̣ὐ̣τ̣ὸ̣ς [ἐπίστ]α[ται]; here we can alternatively supplement [ἐπιστά-]||μενον as in *P.Tebt.* II 385, 23 (Tebtynis, 117 CE): π[α]ρέξεται ὁ Ἥρων τὸν [π]αῖδα ἐ̣π̣[ιστάμ]ε̣ν̣ον ἐ̣[ν]τ̣ε̣[λ]ῆ̣.
[πᾶσαν ἐν|τελ]ῶς̣: cf. *P.Fouad* 37, 1 (Oxyrhynchos, 48 CE): τὴν λινυφικὴν (l. λινουφικὴν) τῶν καθημένων τέχνην πᾶσαν ἐντελῶς.

9–10. εὐορκοῦν[τι μέν μοι εὖ] | [εἴ]ῃ, ἐπιορκοῦντ̣ι δ̣ὲ̣ [τὰ ἐναντία.]: this expression in the liability clause of the oath in the Roman period is attested only in the first century from 3 BCE to 90 CE; its restoration in the lacuna of *P.Col.* VIII 222, 31–33 (Oxyrhunchos, 160/1 CE) was correctly rejected by Packman (1994, p. 208).

91. Marriage Contract

P.Fouad inv. 031 | w 8.5 × h 14 cm | 15.8.29 CE
Ibion Argaiou, Arsinoite

Upper and right edges are largely intact. Above the first line is a margin of about 1.5 cm. The preserved lines of writing run up to the right edge. The left margin is lost along with a portion of approximately five letters from the beginning of each line. Starting from line 18 a portion of about 10 letters of the right side is missing, but these can be restored with certainty. The papyrus was folded horizontally, from the upper side downwards, as shown by the increasing width between the folds. Two smaller fragments in the same envelope constitute the lower part of the same document and include lines 20–22. Then the papyrus breaks off. The back is blank.

The papyrus, dated to the fifteenth year of the reign of Tiberius, preserves a marriage contract in the form of a dowry receipt. It is one of the earliest such documents from Roman Egypt, preceded only by *PSI* I 36a of 11–13 CE.[1] The agreement is written in the form of a *homologia*, in which the groom acknowledges the receipt of 14 drachmas as a dowry, which is the value (διατίμησις) of a woman's chiton. The agreement is made between the groom and the father of the bride, who is the provider of the dowry.[2] The groom Patynis, the bride Taopis and the bride's father Paes all bear pure Egyptian names; Patinas' father may have had a Greek name (see lines 4–5). The receipt was written on the 22nd of Mesore in the 15th year of Tiberius at Ibion Argaiou, a village in the Polemon meris in the Arsinoite nome.

→ [ἔτους π]εντεκαιδεκάτου Τιβερίου Καίσαρος Σεβαστοῦ
[μηνὸς] Ὑ̣περβερεταίου δευτέρᾳ καὶ εἰκάδει Μεσουρὴ
[κβ ἐν] Ἰ̣βίωνι Ἀργαίου τῆς Πολέμωνος μερίδος
[τοῦ Ἀρσ]ινοείτου νομοῦ. ὁμολογεῖ Πατῦνεις Μελ-
[. . . . .] Πέρσης τῆς ἐπιγονῆς ὡς ἐτῶν τριάκοντα
[. . . . .] μελίχρως οὐλὴ ἀν[τι]κ̣νημίῳ ἀριστερῷ Παῆ
[. . . . .]ν̣ος ὡς ἐτῶν τεσσαράκοντα πέντε μέσος με̣-
[λίχρῳ] οὐλὴ δακτύλῳ δευτέρῳ χειρὸς δεξιᾶς ——
[ἔχειν] π̣αρ' αὐτοῦ διὰ χειρὸς ἐκξ οἴκου ὑπὲρ τῆς ἑαυ⟨τοῦ⟩
[θυγατ]ρὸς Ταώπιος φέρνην ἀργυρίου δραχμ[ὰς]
[δέκα τ]έσσαρες, αἵ εἰσιν διατίμησις κιτῶνος γυ-
[ναικ]ε̣ίου· συνβιούτωσαν οὖ\ν/ ἀλλήλοις Πατῦνις
[καὶ Τα]ῶπις ἀμεμψιμοιρήτως· ἐὰν δὲ διαφορᾶ(ς)
[αὐτοῖ]ς γενομένης χωρίζωνται ἀπ' ἀλλήλων,

1. This form was the routine scheme in marriage documents from the Arsinoite nome. A list of all published dowry receipts is provided in Yiftach-Firanko 2003, pp. 17–18.
2. For dowry providers see, Yiftach-Firanko 2003, pp. 276–280; he lists 15 instances in which the father provides the dowry.

[ἀπο]δ̣ό̣τωι ὁ Πατοῖνις τῷ Παῆ, ἐὰν δὲ οὗτος μὴ
[περιῇ,] τῇ Ταώπι τὰς τῆς φερνῆ⟨ς⟩ ἀργυρίου δραχμὰ`ς´
[δέκα] τέσσαρες, ἐπὶ μὲν τῆς ἀπο̣π̣ο̣μ̣π̣ῆς παρα-
[χρῆ]μ̣α, ἐπὶ δὲ τῆς ἑκουσίου ἀπαλ̣[λαγῆς ἐν]
[ἡμέρ]α̣ις τριάκοντα, ἀφ' ἧ̣ς ἐὰν ἀ[παιτηθῇ. ἐὰν]
[δὲ] μὴ ἀποδῷ κ̣α̣θ' ἃ̣ γέγρ̣α̣π̣τα[ι, ἀποτεισάτω]
[παρα]χρῆμα μεθ' ἡμιολ̣ίας, [τῆς πράξεως οὔ-]
[σης ἢ τ]ῷ̣ Παῆ ἤ, μὴ π̣[εριόντος, τῇ Ταώπι]
- -

2 l. εἰκάδι | Μεσου$ρ^{η}$; l. Μεσορὴ || **4** l. Ἀρσινοΐτου || **7** μέσος: nom. for dat. || **9** l. ἐξ || **11** l. τέσσαρας | χιτῶνος; χιτων ex χιτως corr. || **12** l. συμβιούτωσαν || **13** διαφο$ρ^{α}$ || **16** δραχμ$α^{ς}$ || **17** l. τέσσαρας

TRANSLATION

The fifteenth year of Tiberius Caesar Augustus, on the twenty second of the month Hyperberetaios, Mesore 22, in Ibion Argaiou in the meris of Polemon of the Arsinoite nome. Patynis son of Melas (?), Persian of the *epigone*, thirty... years old, [middle sized], with honey-colored complexion, with a scar on the left shin, acknowledges to Paes [son of NN], forty five years old, middle-sized, with honey-colored complexion, with a scar on the second finger of his right hand, to have received from him from hand to hand, out of the house, on behalf of his daughter Taopis a dowry of fourteen silver drachmae, equaling the value of a woman's chiton. Accordingly let Patynis and Taopis live together with one another in contentment, but if disagreement should develop between them and they should separate from one another, Patynis must return to Paes or, if he does not survive, to Taopis the fourteen drachmas of the dowry, immediately in the case of repudiation, and in the case of voluntary separation within 30 days from the day on which the demand was made. If he fails to pay as has been written, let him pay as a penalty what he owes increased by one half, the right of execution resting with Paes or, if he does not survive, with Taopis...

COMMENTARY

1. Μεσουρή: there is a small vertical stroke between the *omikron* and *rho* that resembles a *ypsilon*. Written in this way the name of the month is not common in the Arsinoite; it occurs only once in an ostracon from Narmouthis (*P.Narm.* 26, 5). Other attestations of the same spelling come from different localities.

3. Ἰβιὼν Ἀργαίου (TM Geo 882): of the 41 texts in which the name of this village is attested, only one preserves a transaction that took place there, namely *SB* XXIV 16174 (155 CE), a contract for a sale of a donkey. The village is tentatively identified with the modern-day Tell el-Maraka, between Medinet el-Nehas (Magdola) and Kom el-Khamsini (Berenikis Thesmophorou), see Rathbone 1996, p. 54 and map on p. 50; Vandorpe 1991.

4. Πατῦνεις: the name is written Πατοῖνις in line 15, for the interchange of υ and οι, see Gignac 1981, pp. 197–199. Patynis is a frequently attested personal name in the papyri, especially in the Ptolemaic period. It means "Der (des Herrn) von Tebtynis" and is a variant of Papnebtynis, see *Dem. Nam.* 365 and 431.

4–5. Possibly Μέλ|[ανος].

5. The designation *Persês tês epigonês* in the Roman period is used till about 150 CE to label debtors in various types of contracts; its exact meaning is still obscure. It allowed the creditor to take special measures of execution in case the debtor failed to meet his contractual obligations. For a discussion of the significance as well as the geographical and chronological span of this designation, especially in marriage agreements, see Yiftach-Firanko 2003, pp. 237–240, with bibliography.

5–6. τριάκοντα | [. . . . .]: in the lacuna, either a number or a physical description. In the former case, [πέντε] is likely owing to the common practice of age-rounding, in the latter [μέσος] because of the size of the gap. Cf. line 7 πέντε μέσος. On age-rounding, see Duncan-Jones 1977; Scheidel 1996b (p. 25, n. 2 for further bibliography); Scheidel 1996a. For descriptions of a person's physical characteristics, see Caldara 1924, Hübsch 1968. 30+ years as age of the husband is rather higher than the median male age at first marriage as shown by census returns (see Bagnall, Frier 1994, p. 116).

6. Παῆ: the same dative form (not Παῆτι) in line 15; cf. genitive Παοῦ in *PSI* VI 626 v., 21 (Philadelphia, 263–229 BC). For this name, see *Dem. Nam.*, p. 397: "*Der des Anfangs*; bzw. *Der an der Spitze* (?)."

7–8. μέσος με̣|[λίχρῳ]: the final sigma of μέσος is written with a looped slightly concave bar which extends to the next letter (similar to the final sigma of ἐπιγονῆς in line 5). Since μέσος is nominative for dative, perhaps one should restore με̣|[λίχρως]. The ε at the edge appears to have been written *ex corr.*

9. ἐκξ οἴκου: for the spelling κξ instead of ξ, cf. Gignac 1981, pp. 140–141.

9–10. ὑπὲρ τῆς ἑαυ⟨τοῦ⟩ | [θυγατ]ρὸς Ταώπιος: this phrase usually has ἐπί, but for ὑπέρ, cf. e.g. *P.Mich.* V 343, 2. There is no available space at the beginning of line 10 for ὑπὲρ τῆς ἑαυ|[τοῦ θυγατ]ρός.

10. For the name Taopis, meaning "she of the Nile", see *Dem. Nam.*, p. 1203. It is mainly attested in the Arsinoite, especially at Tebtynis.

11. κιτῶνος: the scribe seems to have first written χιτως, then converted the *sigma* to a *nu*, and then added ος. For the spelling κιτῶνος instead of χιτῶνος (mute instead of aspirate), see Gignac 1981, p. 94. A *chiton* as *pherne* has a valuation of 20 drachmas in the marriage contract in the form of a bank draft, *P.Mich.* XV 700, 9 (Karanis, 143 CE). Usually marriage agreements record the receipt of the cloth and mention the valuation *dia/syntimesis*. Here the groom acknowledges the receipt of the money and equates it with the value of a *chiton*. The same applies, e.g., to *P.Stras.* IV 237, 18–19 (Ptolemais Euergetis, 142 CE): δ̣ρ̣[αχμὰς εἴκ]ο̣σι̣ [τ]ε̣σ̣σαρες (l. τέσσαρας), αἵ εἰσι δακτύλια̣; and *P.IFAO* I 30, 10–11 (Arsinoite, 138–160 CE): ἀργυρίου δρα[χμὰς ἑκατὸν οὔσ]α̣ς [τιμὴν κτλ. For clothes as *pherne* and *parapherna*, see Yiftach-Firanko 2003, pp. 161–164, and pp. 306–309.

12–13. συνβιούτωσαν οὖ\`ν´ ἀλλήλοις Πατῦνις | [καὶ Τα]ῶπις ἀμεμψιμοιρήτως: this clause is attested mainly in the cases of pre-existing marriages from the Arsinoite; see *P.Mich.* V 340, 39–40 (Tebtynis, 45–6 CE); *BGU* I 251, 4–5 (Soknopaiou Nesos, 81 CE); *CPR* I 28, 4–5 (Ptolemais Euergetis, 110 CE); *P.Bodl.* I 61d, 6–7 (Arsinoite (?), II CE).

13–14. ἐὰν δὲ διαφορᾶ(ς)...: the same formula occurs in marriage agreements from the Arsinoite throughout the Roman Period; see *BGU* I 252, 7 (Ptolemais Euergetis, 98 CE); *SB* XII 10924, 15–16 (Theadelphia, 114 CE); *P.IFAO* I 30, 22–23 (Arsinoite, 138–160 CE); *BGU* IV 1045 = *M.Chr.* 282, 21–22 (Alabanthis, 154 CE); *P.Bour.* 15, 11 (Arsinoite, II CE); *SPP* XX 15 = *CPR* I 27 = *M.Chr.* 289, 16–17 (Ptolemais Euergetis, 190 CE); *SB* XVI 12334, 1–2 (Philadelphia, II CE); *P.Hamb.* III 220, 11–14 (Ptolemais Euergetis?, 223/4 CE).

16. δραχμά\`ς´: the scribe seems first to have written δραμα\`ς´ and corrected this by superimposing a χ on the μ.

17–19. Thirty days is the norm in marriage agreements of the first century CE, later, both thirty and sixty days are attested; for the circumstances of the divorce (ἀποπομπή and ἀπαλλαγή) and the rules governing the return of each category of the dowry (*pherne*, *parapherna*, and *prosphora*), see Yiftach-Firanko 2003, pp. 208–210.

21. μεθ̣' ἡμιολ̣ίας: if there is a delay in the return of a dowry, it is "increased by one half" also in *BGU* I 251, 7 (Soknopaiou Nesos, 81 CE); *CPR* I 236, 9 (Soknopaiou Nesos, 81–96 CE). In *P.Mich.* V 340, 57 (Tebtynis, 45/46 CE) interest is also added: μεθ' ἡμιολίας καὶ τόκων. See in general Lewis 1944, pp. 126–139; Taubenschlag 1944 (ed. 1955), pp. 345–347; Wolff 2002, pp. 91–92. For the *hemiolia* in marriage contracts, see Yiftach-Firanko 2003, pp. 210–211, 233. See also Markiewicz 2006 for the Pharaonic origin of the 50% increase in loans.

For the *praxis* provision in general, see Wolff 1941; Dieter 1964. For the *praxis* clause specifically in marriage contracts, see Yiftach-Firanko 2003, pp. 231–237.

22. π̣[εριόντος: for the genitive absolute of περίειμι in the *praxis* provision of a parallel document, cf., e.g., *P.Ryl.* II 154, 32–34 (Bakchias, 66 CE): γει[νο]μένης τῆς πράξ[ε]ως τῶν κατὰ τὴν συνγραφὴν τῶι Σισόϊτι ἤ, μὴ περιόν̣[το]ς̣, τῆι Θαϊσαρί[ωι] καὶ τοῖς [παρ' α]ὐτῆς. The *praxis* clause is otherwise constructed with ἐάν and the subjunctive, as in *P.Mich.* V 340, 57–59 (Tebtynis, 45–46 CE): γινομένης τῷ Διδύμῳ, ἐὰν δὲ μὴ περιῇ, τῇ θυγατρὶ Ἡρακλείᾳ τῆς πράξεως.

92. Mandate Concerning a Debt

P.Fouad inv. 134 — w 6.6 × h 9 cm — II CE
Oxyrhynchos

None of the margins of this mutilated papyrus are preserved, and the beginnings and ends of most lines are lost. But a continuous text can be reconstructed on the basis of attested formulas and the fact that a few lines are complete on the left (lines 12 and 14) or the right (lines 3, 18 and 21). The hand is a slow semi-cursive with few ligatures. The writing on recto runs along the fibers. The verso has a docket written along the fibers. Its writing thus runs perpendicular to the text on the front.

The papyrus records a mandate concerning a private matter, a well-represented type of document from Roman Egypt.[1] Technical terms for this type of document, in actual agreements, are σύστασις, συστατικόν and ἀποσυστατικόν. The term σύστασις was exclusively used in Oxyrhynchos, while συστατικόν occurs in documents from the Arsinoite, Alexandria and the Great Oasis. The latter term also appears in *P.Oxy.* III 509 and *BGU* IV 1093, both found in Oxyrhynchos, although both pertain to legal matters in Alexandria. The term ἀποσυστατικόν turns up only once in the actual agreements (*SB* XVI 12278, 7), and once together with ἐπιτροπική (*BGU* I 300 V°, Arsinoite, 148 CE).[2] Some agreements for mandate, however, do not use any of the aforementioned terms, but rather refer to the type of document with which the agreement was formulated: χειρόγραφον,[3] ὁμολογία,[4] ἐπίσταλμα,[5] συνχώρησις.[6] Later, in the early fourth century, the terms for "mandate" were replaced by ἐντολή; see Passoni Dell'Acqua 1982, (*P.Anag.* =*SB* XVI 12278), p. 134, with a list of documents. Below I provide an updated version to that list. It includes all agreements in which the operative verb is συνίστημι or ἀποσυνίστημι, regardless of the terminology used for "mandate".

P.Fouad 35 (Oxyrhynchos, 48 CE)
SB XX 14071 (Oxyrhynchos, 77CE)
P.Oxy. II 261 = *M.Chr.* 346 (Oxyrhynchos, 55 CE)
P.Oxy. I 94 = *M.Chr.* 344 (Oxyrhynchos, 83 CE)
P.Oxy. LXXXVI 5550 (Oxyrhynchos, 84–90 CE)
SB XX 15033 (Oxyrhynchos, 94 CE)
SB XX 15034 (Oxyrhynchos, end I CE)

1. The main work on representation in papyri is still Wenger 1906, see also Rabel 1933; Rabel 1937; Herrmann 1974, p. 159; *P.Bodl.* 32 introd.; Passoni Dell'Acqua 1982; Solazzi 1924; Hamza 1984; Briguglio 2007, Rupprecht/Kruse 2010.
2. *BGU* I 300 (Arsinoite, 148 CE) uses χειρόγραφον in the body of the agreement, but on the back has both ἀποσυστατικόν and ἐπιτροπική. For ἀποσυστατικὰ γράμματα and ἀποσυστατικόν, see *SB* XX 14585 (Oxyrhynchite (?), 319 CE), 10–11 and 17 respectively.
3. *P.Bodl.* I 31 (Soknopaiou Nesos, 160–176 CE).
4. *P.Oxy.* LXXXVI 5550, the editor supplements [σύστασιν] in line 22 (Oxyrhynchos, 84–90 CE); *P.Mert.* I 18 (Oxyrhynchos, 161 CE).
5. *P.Oxy.* XIV 1643, [6]; 13–14 (298 CE) has ἐπί|[σταλμα.
6. *P.Oxy.* IV 727 (154 CE).

P.Oxy. I 97 (Oxyrhynchos, 115/116 CE)
P.Fam.Tebt. 27 (Tebtynis, 132 CE)
P.Oxy. IV 726 (Oxyrhynchos, 135 CE)
P.Freib. II 9 (Arsinoite, 138–161 CE)
P.Hamb. I 102 (Arsinoite, 138–161 CE)
BGU I 191 (Karanis, 143 CE)
BGU I 300 (Arsinoite, 148 CE)
P.Oxy. IV 727 (Oxyrhynchos, 154 CE)
P.Fouad 36 (Oxyrhynchos, 167 CE)
P.Bodl. 31 (Soknopaiou Nesos, 169–177 CE)
P.Tebt. II 317 = *M.Chr.* 348 (Tebtynis, 174–175 CE)
P.Oxy. III 509 (Oxyrhynchos, II CE)
P.Bodl. 32 (Oasis Magna, 240 CE)
SB I 4653 (Oasis Magna, 240–241 CE)
P.Grenf. II 71 = *M.Chr.* 190 (Oasis Magna, 244–8)
P.Nekr. 13 (Oasis Magna, 250 CE)
BGU IV 1093 (Oxyrhynchos, 265 CE)
P.Oxy. XIV 1642 (Oxyrhynchos, 289 CE)
P.Oxy. XIV 1643 (Oxyrhynchos, 298 CE)
P.Oxy. X 1274 (Oxyrhynchos, III CE)
P.Nekr. 25 = *SB* XIV 16286 (Oasis Magna, *c.* 300 CE)
BGU I 286 (Arsinoite, 306 CE)
SB XX 14585 (Provenance unknown, 319 CE)
SB XVI 12278 = *P.Anag.* p. 136 (Provenance unknown, III–IV CE).

There are two main categories of private mandates. One is the juridical which entitles the mandatary to represent the mandator in judicial procedures and hearings. The other is what we may call business representation, which includes a wide range of different transactions: from a single transaction as a sale of a slave or house to a more general mandate that entitles the mandatary to administer some of or all the mandator's business activities. One contract at least combines both categories (*P.Fouad* 36). In addition, there is a small, but distinctive, group of papyri from the Oasis Magna that are related to the process of the publication (δημοσίωσις) of documents in Alexandria, but that follow a different formula.[7] I here exclude cases of appointing a representative for officials or for liturgical duties such as the collection of taxes, e.g., *P.Fay.* 34 (Theadelphia, 161 CE) and *P.Vind.Sijp.* 17 (Arsinoite, 181/192 CE).

7. Bagnall 1997. The texts there discussed have now been republished as *P.Nekr.* 4, 6 and 10.

The present agreement is written in the form of a *homologia*. It is drafted ἐν ἀγυιᾷ, "in the street", i.e. at the *agoranomeion*.[8] The mandators are (at least) three sisters. We know the full identification of only one of them: Aristous alias Apollonarion daughter of Herakleides, but another was a certain Demetria, while information about the third is entirely missing. They appoint a man (full name lost, but grandson of a certain Dionysios) as a mandatary to recover a sum of money from a woman called Antonia Kyria. That money had been owed by her deceased father, Antonius Asklepiades, to the deceased father of the mandators, and Antonia Kyria is now responsible to pay back her father's debt. The mandatary is entitled to demand (ἀπαιτεῖν) that money and, if he recovers it (ἀπολάμβανειν?), to issue a receipt (ἀποχὴν προιέσθαι) or, in case of failure of repayment, to sue Antonia (προσέρχεσθαι κατ' αὐτῆς) on condition that he give to the mandators whatever he receives.

The closest parallels to the present document—in formulation, but not subject matter—are *P.Fouad* 35 (Oxyrhynchos, 48 CE) and *P.Oxy*. I 94 (Oxyrhynchos, 83 CE.). The present case is perhaps similar to the agreement, which had been modified in the draft *P.Oxy*. III 509 (Oxyrhynchos, II CE), where the power of collecting the debt is modified because the creditor had already received the debt and power of attorney is granted only to issue the receipt. Appointing a *procurator* for collecting debts is also recorded in *SB* XX 15033 (Oxyrhynchos, 94 CE).

The date of the transaction is not preserved, but since we already know two of the contracting parties from other papyri, the present one can be dated somewhat more closely than by paleographical considerations alone. One of the creditors, Aristous, is fully identified in the will *P.Oxy*. III 494, written in 156 CE and opened in 165 CE. There we encounter her as Ἀριστοῦς ἡ καὶ Ἀπολλωνάριον Ἡρακλείδου τοῦ Διονυσίου τοῦ καὶ Ἀκουσιλάου μητρὸς Ἡραίδος Ἀλεξάνδρου. And we also learn that she was the wife of the testator Ἀκουσίλαος Δείου τοῦ Διονυσίου τοῦ καὶ Ἀκουσιλάου, who was also her cousin through her father's side, to whom she begot a son named Dios.[9] The husband of Aristous was 48 years old at the time that the will was written, in 156 CE, but Aristous age is not specified. If Aristous was still a minor in our document (line 10), we can roughly date the present papyrus to the second quarter of the second century CE.[10]

That we are dealing with families of the upper class of Oxyrhynchos is evident from what we know about the debtor Ἀντωνία Κυρία ἡ καὶ Ἀσκληπίας. She is attested only once in *P.Oxy*. III 498, which is palaeographically dated to the second century CE (see comm. on lines 5–6). In this document Antonia draws up a contract through her business manager (ἐπίτροπος) Apollonios with two stone-cutters to provide different sizes and types of stone blocks for the construction

8. For the stereotypical idiom ἐν ἀγυιᾷ, which was exclusively used in documents from Oxyrhynchos, to mean that the agreement was drafted at the *agoranomeion*, see Wolff 1978, pp. 15–16; Turner 2007, pp. 141–154, esp. p. 144. On the *agoranomeion*, see Raschke 1974; Alston 2002, p. 188.
9. The family of Akousilaos has been already identified by the editor of *P.Oxy*. LXXII 4875 (see lines 1–2 comm., with a family stemma on p.102). Demetria sister of Aristous should now be included in the stemma. The grandfather's name of the mandatary Dionysios (line 2) may indicate that he is a member of the same family.
10. The reading of the name Aristous alias Apollonarion in *P.Worp* 22, 6–7 (Oxyrhynchos, II CE?), whom the editor suggests is our Aristous, had been justifiably rejected in the reedition by Borrelli 2016, pp. 20–21.

of her (new?) house in the quarter of the Garden of Pammenes, where a number of the elite are known to have lived.[11]

Asklepias' father, Antonius Asklepiades, furthermore, is probably the same person attested in *SB* XVI 12553, 3 (Oxyrhynchos, II–III CE) as the purchaser of several arouras of vineland in Oxyrhynchos for one talent and three thousand drachmas. If this identification is correct, one should read Ἀντωνίῳ Ἀσκληπιάδῃ̣ instead of Ἀντωνίῳ Ἀσκληπιάδ[ου],[12] and the date of the document can be pushed back and narrowed down to the late first or early second century.

\- -

→ [. . . . .] δι . . [. .] . [. . . .] . . . . . . [. . . . . τοῦ]
[Διο]ν̣υσίου μητρὸς Σαραποῦτος πάντε̣ς̣ [ἀπ']
[Ὀξυ]ρ̣ύγχων π[ό]λεως, ἐν ἀγυιᾷ, συνεστακέ̣-
[ναι α]ὐ̣τὸν κα[τὰ] τήνδε τὴν ὁμολογίαν ἀπ̣[αι-]
[τήσ]ο̣ντα Ἀντωνίαν Κυρίαν τὴν καὶ̣ [Ἀσ<κλη>-]
[πι]ά̣δα ἃ προφέρονται οἱ ὁμολογοῦντες ὀ̣[φεί-]
[λ]ε̣σθαι ὑπὸ τοῦ μετηλλαχότος αὐτῆς π̣[α-]
[τρ]ὸς Ἀντωνίου Ἀσκληπ̣ι̣άδου, οὗ γεγονέ̣ν̣[αι]
[αὐ]τὴν κληρονόμον, τῷ̣ μετηλλαχότι τῷ̣[ν]
[ἀφηλ]ίκων̣ [π]α̣τ̣ρ̣[ὶ] τ̣ῷ̣ π̣ρογεγραμμένῳ Ἡ[ρα-]
[κλείδῃ̣, ἃ]ς δεδ̣[άνεικε αὐ]τ̣ῷ̣ [ὁ] Ἡρακλείδης κ̣α̣[τὰ]
χειρόγραφον [δραχ]μ̣ὰς Α καὶ̣ τ̣ό̣κ̣ους, κ̣α̣ὶ̣ [ἔτι],
[ε]ἰ μὲν ἀπολά̣β̣ο̣[ι αὐ]τ̣ά̣ς, ἀποχὴν προησόμε[νον],
εἰ δὲ μή γε, προ`σ̣´ελευ<σ>όμ̣[ε]νον κατ' αὐτῆς [ὡ̣ς]
[δ]έ̣ον ἐστί, καὶ π̣ά̣ν̣τ̣α̣ ἐπιτελέσοντα ὅσα [καὶ]
[τοῖς ὁμο]λογοῦσι⟨ν⟩ ἔξεστιν. εὐδοκεῖν γὰρ [ἐ]π̣[ὶ]
[τούτοις], ἐφ' ᾧ τὰ προστελο̣ύμενα αὐτῷ ὑ̣π' α̣[ὐ-]
[τῆς ἀποδ]ώ̣σει τοῖς ὁμολογοῦσι, τῆς πίστεως
[περὶ αὐτὸ]ν οὔσης. κυρία ἡ ὁμολογία. (*m.* 2) Ἀρισ-
[τοῦς ἡ κα]ὶ Ἀπολλωνάρι̣ο̣ν̣ Ἡρακλείδου συν-
[έστησα σὺν καὶ τῇ ἀδε]λφῇ μου Δημητρίᾳ̣
[. . . . . καὶ τῇ ἀδ]ελφῇ μου [. . . . . .]

\- -

Back:

→ Φαρμ(οῦθι) ιθ ὁμολ(ογία) Ἀριστοῦτ(ος) [?]

3 αγυϊα || Back: Φαρ^{μ} | ομο^{λ} | αριστου^{τ}

11. See Ri. Alston, Ro. Alston 1997, p. 212, n. 60.
12. For a digital image of this papyrus, see: http://ub–prod01–imgs.uio.no/OPES/jpg/1613r.jpg.

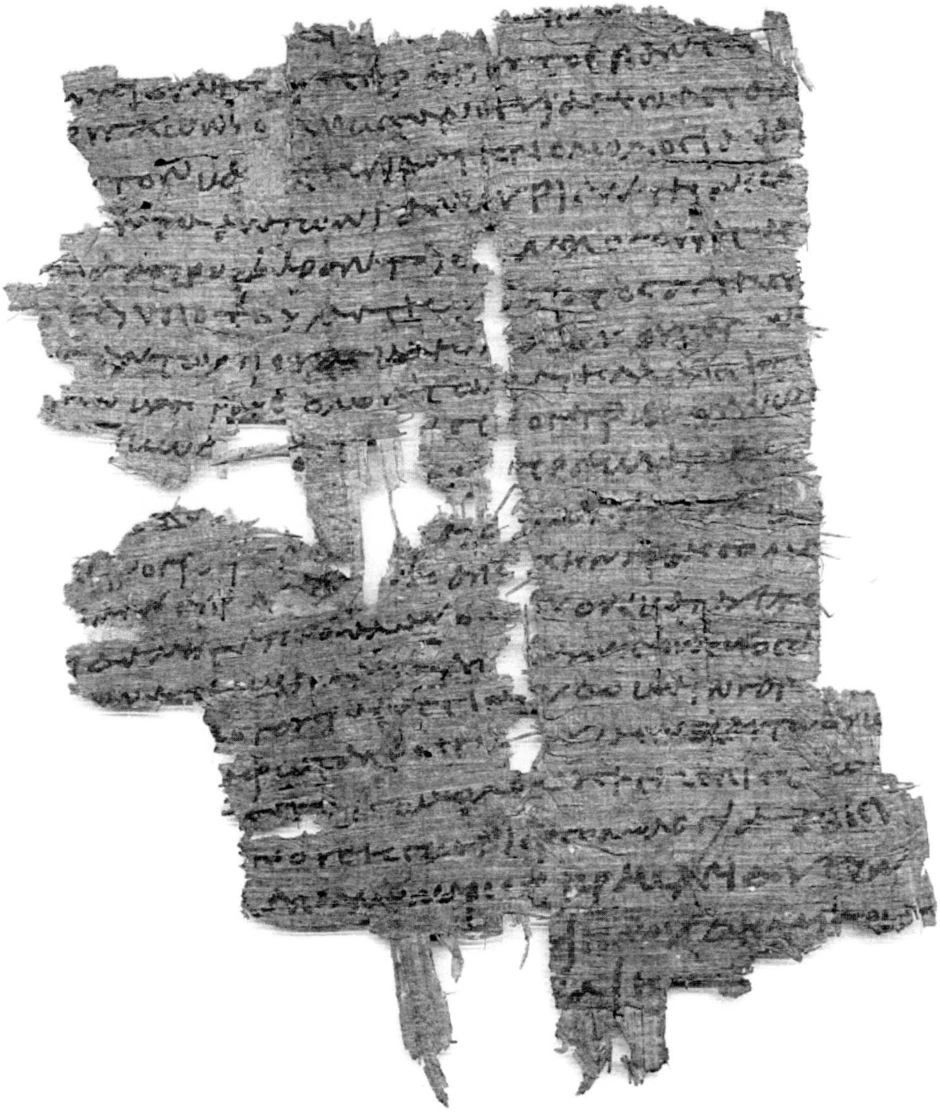

[92 recto]

[92 verso]

TRANSLATION

… to NN son of NN] grandson of Dionysios, his mother being Sarapous, all from Oxyrhynchos, in the street, acknowledge that they have appointed him, according to this agreement, as mandatary to demand from Antonia Kyria alias Asklepias, what they claim to be owed by her deceased father Antonius Asklepiades, of whom she has become heir, to the minors' deceased father, the aforementioned Herakleides, what Herakleides has lent him according to a *cheirographon*, 1000 drachmas with interest, and further, if he collects them, issue a receipt, but if not, sue her in the proper way, and to do everything which are in the power of the acknowledgers (the mandators), for they agree on these terms, on condition that whatever is paid to him by her, he gives back to the acknowledgers (the mandators), because of the obligations of good faith incumbent on him. The agreement is valid. I Aristous alias Apollonarion appointed as representative [together with?] my sister Demetria [ ] and? my sister…

Back: Pharmouthi 19, agreement of Aristous…

COMMENTARY

1. The formula is continuing from the previous lost lines, and should have run parallel to e.g. *P.Fouad* 35 (Oxyrhynchos, 48 CE) which starts with the date and location followed by the ὁμολογεῖ formula. Here we should expect the name of the mandatary in the dative.

5–6. Ἀντωνίαν Κυρίαν τὴν καὶ [Ἀσ<κλη>]||[πι]ά̣δα: restored with *P.Oxy.* III 498, 1–2: Ἀντωνίᾳ Ἀσκληπιάδι τῇ καὶ Κυρίᾳ, where the Greek names appear in reverse order. For persons bearing double name NNa alias NNb sometimes referred to as NNb alias NNa; cf. Broux 2014, s.nn. Aurelius Achilleus alias Isidoros (TM Per 136397) and Agathos Daimon alias Didymos (TM Per 120714). This can happen even in one and the same document, cf. Broux 2014, s.nn. Akousilaos alias Mysthes (TM Per 166693) Alexandra alias Sempronia (TM Per 129506). Since there is hardly enough room for [Ἀσκλη-] at the end of line 5, the omission of a syllable, [Ἀσ<κλη>]||[πι]ά̣δα, has been assumed. This occurs not infrequently when a word is divided at the end of a line.

14. προ`σ´ελευ<σ>όμ̣[ε]νον: the verb has its technical legal sense "to appear before a tribunal" in combination with κατά often in reports of court proceedings; cf. *PSI* I 41, 18 (Antinopolis, IV CE): προσῆλθον τῷ δικαστηρίῳ κατ' αὐτοῦ. Also προέρχομαι would be acceptable, cf., e.g., *P.Rein.* II 96, 2–4 (Hermopolite, 133–137 CE): προ[ερχ]ομένη ἐπὶ τοῦ κρατίστου ἡγεμόνος Πετ̣ρ̣ω̣νίου Μ̣αμερτείνου κ̣α̣τ̣[ὰ] Ν̣ω̣ρβανοῦ Παρο̣υ̣ . .

ἀποχὴν προησόμε[νον]: the right of the mandatary to issue the receipts is attested in *BGU* I 300, 6–7 (Arsinoite, 148 CE): ἀποχὰς προησόμενον αὐ̣τοῖς ἐκ το[ῦ] ἐμοῦ ὀνόματος, see also *P.Oxy.* III 509, 13–14 (Oxyrhynchos, II CE): τὴν ἀποχὴ[ν] ἐκδοθῆναι.

15–16. καὶ πάντα ἐπιτελέσοντα γὰρ [ἐπὶ] | [τοῖς ὁμο]λογοῦσι⟨ν⟩ ἔξεστιν: for a similar formula, but with ἐξῆν rather than ἔξεστιν, cf. *P.Oxy.* I 97, 16–19 (Oxyrhynchos, 116 CE): καὶ πάντα ἐπιτελέσοντα καθὰ καὶ τῷ ὁμ[ο]λογοῦντι ἐξῆν, εὐδοκεῖν γὰρ ἐπὶ τούτοις. κυρία ἡ ὁμολογία, and in *SB* XX 15034, 9–13 (Oxyrhynchos, I CE): καὶ πάντα ἐπιτελέσοντας καθὰ καὶ τῇ ὁμολογούσῃ ἐξῆν, εὐδοκεῖν γὰρ ἐπὶ τούτοις. κυρία ἡ ὁμολογία. The formula, with ἔξεστιν, is attested in *BGU* I 300, 7–8 (Arsinoite, 148 CE): καὶ πάντα τῇ ἐπι[τρο]πῇ ἀνήκοντα ἐπιτελέσοντα, καθὰ καὶ ἐμοὶ παρόντ[ι ἔ]ξεστιν. Other variations are also found in *SB* XX 14071, 15–17 (Oxyrhynchos, 77 CE): καὶ τὰ ἄλλα ἐπιτελέσοντα καθὰ καὶ αὐτ[ῷ] τῶι Τίτωι Φλαουίωι Κλήμετεị παρ[όν]τι ἐξῆν; *P.Oxy.* IV 726, 20–21 (Oxyrhynchos, 134 CE): κ[αὶ] πάντα ἐπιτελέσοντα περὶ τῶν [κ]ατὰ τὴν σύστασιν; *P.Oxy.* IV 727, 14–25 (Oxyrhynchos, 154 CE): πάντα δὲ ἐπιτελεσοντα (l. ἐπιτελέσοντι) καθὰ καὶ αὐτοῖς παροῦσι ἐξῆν; *P.Fouad* 36, 17–18 (Oxyrhynchos, 167 CE): ἐπιτελέσοντα αὐτὸν ὅσα [ἐὰν δέον ᾖ καθὰ καὶ αὐτῇ τῇ συνεστακυίᾳ Σαραπιάδι παρούσῃ ἐξῆν]. I owe the reading of [δ]ẹον ἐστί to Dieter Hagedorn.

18–19. τῆς πίστεως [περὶ αὐτὸ]ν οὔσης: the πίστις clause in the present case concerns the obligation of the mandatary regarding the delivery of whatever he collects to the principal. In mandates it appears only where there is a question of collecting money by the mandatary either through sales or debts or rents, and it comes closely connected to the phrase, which makes it an obligation for the mandatary to deliver whatever sums he collects, cf. *P.Fouad* 35, 11–12 (Oxyrhynchos, 48 CE): ἐφ' ᾧ ἀποκαταστήσει τῇ Θαήσει ἅπαντα, τῆς πίστεως περὶ αὐτὸν οὔσης; *P.Oxy.* I 94, 15–19 (Oxyrhynchos, 83 CE): ἐφ' ᾧ τὴν δοθησομένην αὐτῷ τούτων ἢ τοῦ ἀπ' αὐτῶν πραθησομένου τιμὴν ἀποκαταστείσειν (l. ἀποκαταστήσειν) τῷ Ἀντωνίῳ Πτολεμαίῳ, τῆς πίστεως περὶ αὐτὸν Διονύσ[ι]ον οὔσης. For πίστις in general see Schmitz 1964, Ratzan 2011, pp. 121–169. See also *P.Fouad* 35, 11 comm.; Rupprecht/Kruse 2010, pp. 391–392 for the significance of the πίστις clause in the *systasis* contracts.

The female name Aristous is only attested at Oxyrhynchos from the second to the fourth centuries CE.

20–21. συν|[έστησα σὺν καὶ τῇ ἀδε]λφῇ μου Δημητρίᾳ]: the restoration is illustrative. The same verb, however, is used in the *hypographe* of *P.Oxy.* I 97, 10–21 (Oxyrhynchos, 116 CE): Διογένης Ἀμμωνίου τοῦ Νικάνωρος συνέστησα τὸν ἀδελφὸν. Another possible restoration is συν|[ωμολόγησα σὺν τῇ ἀδε]λφῇ. In *P.Oxy.* I 97 and *P.Fam.Tebt.* 27 (Tebtynis, 132 CE) the *hypographe* of the mandators is followed by that of the mandatary.

93. Receipt for Payments by a Bank

P.Fouad inv. 227 | w 11.3 × h 19.5 cm | 105/6 CE
Lykopolis (?)

The right side of the papyrus has been lost in consequence of a break along a vertical fold. Text is also lost at the top, left and bottom, although remnants of the last line of writing and some of the lower margin are preserved. The dating formula in lines 5–7 makes it possible to estimate the number of the missing letters in the preserved part of the body of the text (up to line 10). From line 11 downwards (subscriptions) it is not possible to offer accurate estimates. The back is blank.

This is a receipt dated to the ninth year of Trajan, i.e. 105/6 CE, and addressed to a municipal banker (πολιτικὸς τραπεζίτης) whose name is lost in the lacuna, but his father's name is Apollonios. The recipients (at least sixteen men) acknowledge the receipt of a certain amount of money from Flavius Apollonius the *strategos* of a certain nome (see below for discussion of the provenance of this document).

The receipt is penned in the semi-cursive hand of one of the recipients, Didymos son of Ptolemaios, and signed by at least fifteen other persons, of whom only one, Didymion son of Zeudis (lines 20–24), was illiterate (ἀγράμματος) and signed through a *hypographeus*.

The amount due per month is sixteen drachmas, therefore one can speculate that the recipients were likewise sixteen in number, making the share of each of them one drachma per month. The total sum is lost in the lacuna in lines 8–9, but the number eight from what must be the same sum is visible in line 22. If we multiply 16 drachmas in order to get a number of drachmas ending in 8, we have a choice between 48 drachmas (= 3 months) or 128 drachmas (= 8 months). Since the payment is for a number of months in the same year beginning with the month Pharmouthi (line 5), the number of months can only be 3.

The information that described the purpose of the payment is lost in the gap in lines 4–5. The payment seems to be owed in accordance with an agreement (ὁμολογία), perhaps made through the same bank, see line 21. It was probably for a service that the recipients had performed for the *strategos* or for the price of commodities that they provided to him for the specified period. The *strategos* could be involved in payments for private as well as public services. In *P.Oxy.* XVII 2138 of 219 CE, a greengrocer acknowledges to the *strategos* of the Hermopolite nome that he has received from his freedman the value of the vegetables that he supplied to the *strategos* during a period of four months. The payment was made through a private bank. Other receipts were also addressed to the *strategos* and not to bankers as, e.g., in *P.Oxy.* LX 4056 (Prosopite, 154/5? CE), where the service—the price of πυρὸς συναγοραστικός—for which the beneficiaries are refunded is public. The fact that the payment in our case is made through a municipal banker suggests that we are dealing with a public matter not a private one.

The text contains our earliest attestation of a municipal bank. This is important, since it is thought that the municipal bank did not exist in the nome capitals until the reforms of Septimius

Severus and the granting of the βουλή in 200 CE.[1] In the present case, we should assume that the service in question was a municipal one, and that it was paid out of the πολιτικὸς λόγος, which existed before the third century.[2] In *P.Oxf.* 2 the *strategos* of the meris of Herakleides orders the *archontes* to pay the wages of transport-work (φόρετρα) due to the camel-keepers of Soknopaiou Nesos and Karanis out of the municipal fund; the editor (p. 6) rightly excluded the possibility that the purpose of the payment was for the transport of grain destined to Alexandria because the payments in these cases are paid through the public banker.

On the other hand, it is also possible that the πολιτικὸς τραπεζίτης is not equivalent to a municipal banker (πολιτικῶν χρημάτων τραπεζίτης), but rather a synonym for the public banker. It might even mean nothing more than the bank in the city,[3] i.e. a metropolis.

The probable, though not certain, provenance of the papyrus is Lykopolis. Although most of the personal names are fairly common in the published documentary evidence, the name Lykos in line 14 is a possible indication of Lykopolis as the likely provenance (see also line 16 comm. below, and **97**, 4 comm.). Furthermore, the inventory number of the papyrus falls within the range of papyri that most likely originate from middle Egypt, especially Lykopolis (see the introduction, pp. 3–4). Indeed, the immediately following inv. number (228) is an unpublished *tomos synkollesimos* that comprises two census declarations for 159 CE from Lykopolis. Both declarations are addressed to the *laographos* Besas of a certain *amphodon* Γεω()? at Lykopolis. Furthermore, the *strategos* Flavius Apollonius in line 4 of the papyrus could well be the same Apollonius, who is attested as a *strategos* of the Polemon meris of the Arsinoite in the same period,[4] but there could have been two different Apollonii acting as *strategoi* in two different nomes at the same time.

- -

→ [.] .ε̣ρ̣[. . . .] .[. . . .] .α [- - -]
[. . . . .] καὶ Δίδυ̣μ̣[ος Δη]μητρί[ο]υ ο[ἱ] δέκ[α ἓξ . . . .]
[. . . . . .] .ω̣ Ἀπολλωνίου πολιτικῶι τραπεσζε[ίτ̣η . . . . ἀπεσχηκέ-]
[ναι αὐτο]ὺ̣ς παρὰ Φλαυίου Ἀπολλωνίου στρα[τηγοῦ . . . .]
[. . . . .]μ̣ον ἀπ[ὸ] Φαρμοῦθι τοῦ διεληλυθ̣[ότος ὀγδόου ἔτους Αὐτο-]
[κράτορος Κα]ίσαρος Νέρουα Τραιανοῦ Σεβαστοῦ [Γερμανικοῦ Δακικοῦ]
[ἕως Παῦνι τοῦ] αὐτοῦ ὀκδώου ἔτους, μηνῶν [τριῶν ὡς ἑκάστου μηνὸς]
[ἀργυρίου δρ]α̣χ(μὰς) δέκα ἕξ, τὰς συναγομένας ἀργ[υρίου δραχμὰς τεσσαρά-]
[κοντα ὀκτώ. Δί]δυμος Πτολεμαίου ἔγραψα κα[ὶ συνανείρημαι. (ἔτους) θ Αὐτο-]

1. Municipal banks/bankers are usually associated with the reforms of Septimius Severus, and are attested from the third century CE on; cf. Bogaert 2000, pp. 200–201 and the discussion offered by Mitthof in *CPR* XXIII 23, pp. 138–139. Municipal banks/bankers are mainly concerned with payments of taxes, see Bogaert 1997, pp. 121–122.

2. For the πολιτικὸς λόγος (ὁ τῆς πόλεως λόγος), see *P.Sijp.* 21a, 23 comm. It is attested for the mid-second century CE in *P.Oxf.* 2 (Ptolemais Euergetis, 141 CE) and *SB* XIV 11959, 1 (Herakleopolis, 142 CE). For the finances of the *metropoleis* before the reforms of Septimius Severus and the role of the *strategos*, see *P.Oxf.* 2, pp. 5–11.

3. Cf. the tentative reading suggested for *P.Brem.* 46, 2 (Hermopolis?, 110 CE) μ̣[.] . . .π( ) τράπ(εζαν) where the editor suggested the reconstruction μ[η]τ̣ρ̣ο̣π(ολιτικὴν) in reference to a private rather than a municipal bank; cf. also Bogaert 1995, p. 158, n. 120.

4. Whitehorne 2006, p. 37.

[κράτορος Κα]ί̣σ̣αρος Ν̣έρουα Τραιανοῦ Σεβαστοῦ Γ[ερμανικοῦ Δακικοῦ, Month and day]
[(*m.* 2) ....]μος Ἱέρακος συν{σ}α̣νείρημαι ὡς πρ[όκειται ....]
[(*m.* 3) .... σ̣υναν]είρημαι κ̣αθὼς πρόκειται (*m.* 4) Καλ . [..................]
[...... καθὼ]ς̣ πρόκειται (*m.* 5) Ἀπολλώνιος ὁ καὶ Ὀνήσιμ[ος ....]
[(*m.* 6) .... Ἡρ]α̣κλεί(δης) ὁ καὶ Βησᾶς Λύκου συ̣ν̣ανείρημαι καθὼς πρόκ̣[ειται ....]
[(*m.* 7) .... κα]θ̣ὼς πρόκειται (*m.* 8) Ἀ̣ν̣ο̣ύβιο̣ς Πτ̣ο̣λεμαίο̣υ συνανείρη̣[μαι καθὼς πρόκειται ......]
[(*m.* 9) .... συν]α̣νείρημαι καθὼς πρόκ(ειται) (*m.* 10) Ἀπολλώνιος Ἀνδρότιμος συ̣[νανείρημαι ....]
[(*m.* 11) ....] σ̣υ̣ν̣α̣νίρημαι καθὸς πρόκειδαι (*m.* 12) Ἡρακλείδης Ἡ[..................]
[(*m.* 13) ....]ο̣ς ὁ καὶ Βῆσας Ἀπολ̣λωνίου συνανείρ[ημαι καθὼς πρόκειται]
[(*m.* 14) .... συνανείρη]μαι καθὼς [πρό]κειται (*m.* 15) Λέων Διδυμ[...................]
[(*m.* 16) ....] Δ̣ιδυμίω̣ν̣ [Ζε]ύ̣διος ἀνείρημα<ι> κ̣α̣[..................]
[..................] . ην ὠφειλ( ) κ[αθ' ὁμ]ο̣λ̣(ογίαν) γε(γονυῖαν) διὰ τ̣ῆς αὐτῆς [τραπέζης ἀργυρίου]
[δραχμὰς τεσσαράκοντα] ὀ̣κ̣τ̣ὼ̣ καὶ οὐ[δὲν] α̣ὐτῶι ἐγκαλῶι [..................]
[.......... ἔγραψα ὑπὲρ] α̣ὐ̣τοῦ γ[ρ(άμματα) μὴ] εἰδότος. (ἔτους) θ Αὐτ[οκράτορος Καίσαρος]
[.........................] . , [month and day].

3 l. τραπεζίτη || **5** l. διεληλυθότος || **6** l. ὀγδόου || **7** δρ]α̣$^{\chi}$ || **10** passim l. συνανή̣ρημαι || **14** Ἡρ]ακλει¯ || **15** l. καθὼς || **16** l. πρόκειται || **21** ομο$^{\lambda}$

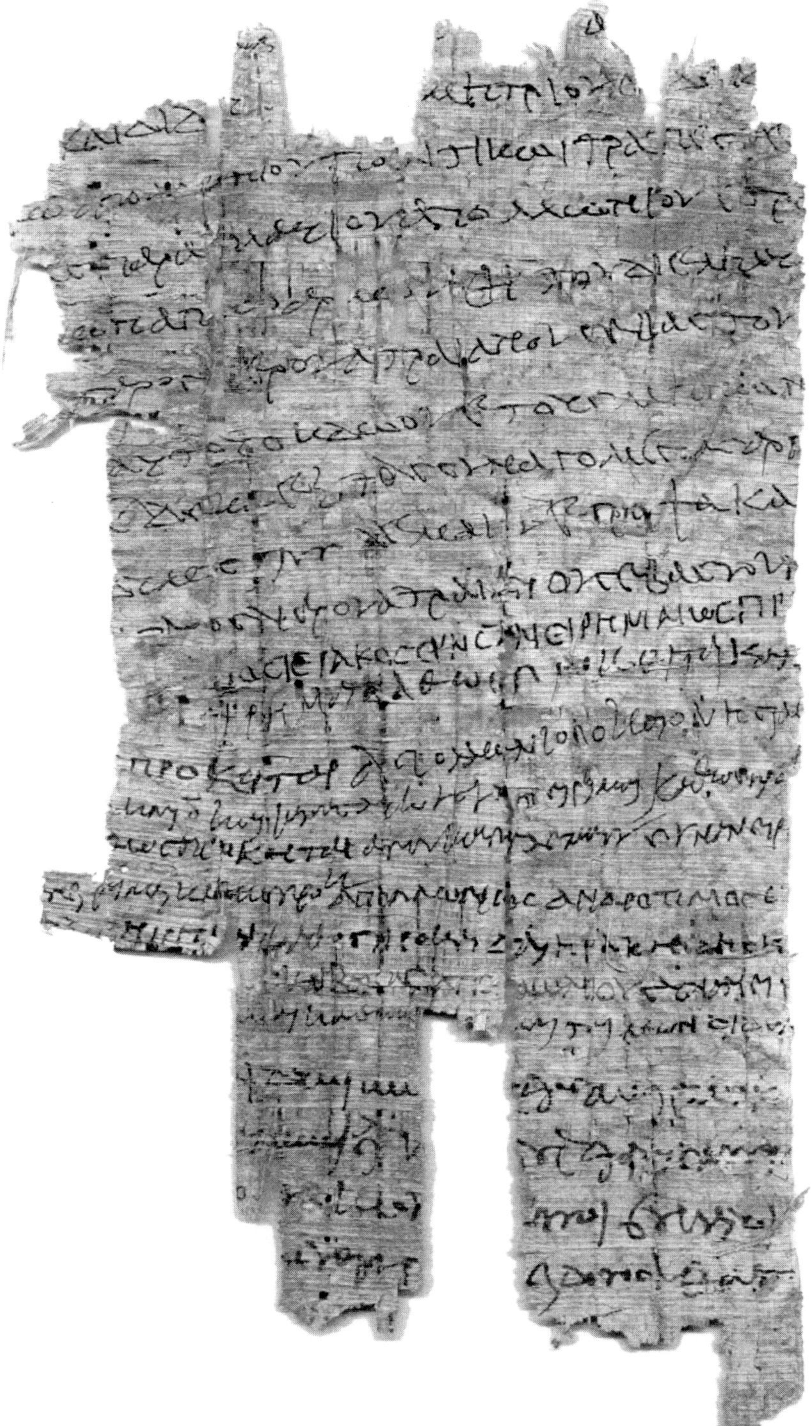

[93]

TRANSLATION

... and Didymos son of Demetrios, the sixteen acknowledge to NN son of Apollonios, the city banker, that they have received from Flavius Apollonius, the *strategos* of... from the month of Pharmouthi of the preceding eighth year of Imperator Caesar Nerva Traianus Augustus Germanicus Dacicus to Pauni of the same eighth year, for three months, making sixteen silver drachmas per month, the sum of forty-eight silver drachmas. I Didymos son of Ptolemaios wrote (the receipt) and have received. The 9th year of Imperator Caesar Nerva Traianus Augustus Germanicus Dacicus, Month and day. I... mos son of Hierax have received as aforesaid. I NN son of NN have received as aforesaid. I Kal... son of NN have received as aforesaid. I Apollonios alias Onesimos son of NN have received as aforesaid. I Herakleides alias Besas son of Lykos have received as aforesaid. I NN son of NN have received as aforesaid. I Anoubios son of Ptolemaios have received as aforesaid. I NN son of NN have received as aforesaid. I Apollonios Androtimos have received as aforesaid. I NN son of NN have received as aforesaid. I Herakleides son of He... have received as aforesaid. I... os alias Besas son of Apollonios have received as aforesaid. I NN son of NN have received as aforesaid. I Leon son of Didym... have received as aforesaid. I Didymion son of Zeudis have received as aforesaid. ... the debt according to the agreement executed through the same bank, forty-eight silver drachmas, and I make no charge against him. I NN son of NN have written for him because he is illiterate. Year 9 of Imperator Caesar..., month and day.

COMMENTARY

3. τραπεσζε[ίτῃ: for the spelling σζ for ζ, see Gignac 1981, pp. 123–124.

7. μηνῶν [τριῶν ὡς ἑκάστου μηνός]: for the restoration of three months, see introd. Instead of ὡς ἑκάστου μηνὸς one might restore the more common ὡς τοῦ μηνὸς, but this renders the line some 2–4 letters shorter than expected; cf. the supplement also suggested for *P.Münch.* III.1 101, 10.

9. Δί]δυμος Πτολεμαίου: persons with this name are attested several times, mostly from the Fayum, but none of them can be identified with the present person.

15–16. Relatively few letters are lost to the right of 15 and to the left of 16. For the names to fit in, there was probably some abbreviation.

16. Ἀπολλώνιος Ἀνδρότιμος: I am inclined to consider this a mistake for nominative followed by a patronymic in genitive rather than a "zeromorph double name", see Broux 2015, pp. 136–140. Apart from the *cognomen* of Tiberius Claudius Androtimus the *strategos* of the Arsinoite for the meris of Herakleides in 66 CE (*P.Mich.* IX 523, 1), and another high official (Claudius Androtimus) in *P.Vind.Worp* 1, 2 (90 CE), the personal name Androtimos is attested for two individuals: Androtimos son of Dios grandson of Dios in *P.Oxy.Census*, 21 (76–100 CE) and Aurelius Androtimus alias Candianus, an *ex-archon* and *dekaprotos*, in *O.Kell.* 5, 4 (259 CE); 10, 5–6 (254 CE); 17, 3–4 (253–259 CE).

20. [Ζε]ύ̣διος: the name Ζεῦδις is very rare; it is attested in this form only in *SB* V 7559 (Tebtynis, 118 CE), and *PSI* X 1117, 3, 9 and 26, with *BOEP* 8.1, p. 2, (Tebtynis, II CE) where the editor reads Ζεύσιος, but examining the photo reveals that the name could well be read Ζεύδιος (Photo available online via PN at http://papyri.info/ddbdp/psi;10;1117. Another variant, Ζεῦθις, is also attested in *P.Phil.* 18, 35 (Philadelphia, II CE).

21. .ην ωφειλ( ): perhaps τ̣ὴν ὠφειλ(ήν), l. ὀφειλήν.

κ[αθ' ὁμ]ο̣λ̣(ογίαν) γε(γονυῖαν) διὰ τ̣ῆς αὐτῆ̣ς [τραπέζης: for documents drawn up by banks see Bogaert 2001, esp. pp. 263–264 for contracts.

23–24. The space allows for a short imperial titulature or one of more usual length but with some of the elements abbreviated.

94. Copy of a Receipt for a Dowry

P.Fouad inv. 280 — w 6.4 × h 10.6 cm — 114–117 CE
Ptolemais Euergetis

The upper left part of a document inscribed along the fibers of the recto in a rapid semi-cursive. Line length of ca. 45 letters can be calculated on the basis of the dating formula in lines 1–2. The back is blank.

The fragment preserves a copy of a notarial contract in which a husband, whose name and patronymic are missing in the lacuna, acknowledges to his wife, by virtue of an unwritten marriage, the receipt of her dowry which consisted mainly, as far as we can tell, of golden jewelry. In the Roman period, it was a common practice in the Arsinoite nome to use a dowry receipt instead of a marriage contract. For a complete list of dowry receipts, see Yiftach-Firanko 2003, pp. 16–18.

Both the husband and the wife are in their fourties, 42 and 48 respectively, and should have been living together for a period of time without written instrument. The wife, as it often happens in longstanding marriages, provides her own dowry.[1] It is not uncommon for wives to be older than husbands as shown by census returns from Roman Egypt where a wife in one case was 8 years older than the husband.[2]

The document is dated to the reign of Trajan. The presence of the adjective Ἄριστος in his titulature dates the document to the years 114–117 CE.[3] The transaction has taken place in Ptolemais Euergetis.

→ ἀντίγρ(αφον) συνγραφῆς. [(ἔτους) . . Αὐτοκράτορος Καίσαρος Νέρουα]
Τραιανοῦ Ἀρίστου Σεβ[αστοῦ Γερμανικοῦ Δακικοῦ μηνὸς Νέου]
Σεβασ(τοῦ) ῑ ἐν Πτολεμ[αΐδι Εὐεργέτιδι τοῦ Ἀρσινοΐτου νομοῦ]
ἐπὶ Ἰουλίας Σεβαστῆς. [ὁμολογεῖ . . . .]
τοῦ Πτολεμαίου το[ῦ καὶ . . . . Πέρσης τῆς ἐπιγονῆς]
ὡ(ς) (ἐτῶν) μβ ἄση(μος) τῇ συνού[σῃ . . . .]
ἀγράφως γ̣υναικὶ̣ [. . . . τοῦ]
Λυσιμάχου ὡ(ς) (ἐτῶν) μη [. . . . μετὰ κυρίου τοῦ]
συνγενοῦς Ζωί[λου τοῦ . . . .]
ἔχειν παρ' αὐτῆς [ἐφ' ἑαυτῇ φερνὴν . . . .]
χρυσοῦ δοκειμ̣ε̣[ίου τετάρτας . . . . αἵ]
[εἰσι δακ]τ̣ύλια ὑέλειν̣[α . . . .]
[καὶ δακτ]ύλειος ὁ[μοίως . . . . γίνονται]
[ἐπὶ τὸ] α̣ὐτὸ αἱ π̣[ροκείμεναι . . . .]

1. For an extended discussion on the unwritten marriage and its various aspects see Yiftach-Firanko 2003, pp. 81–103.
2. Bagnall, Frier 1994, p. 119.
3. More specifically, after 29 August 114 CE, when the 18th year of Trajan started in Egypt. On the use of Ἄριστος = *Optimus* in Trajan's titulature in the papyrological evidence, see the discussion offered by Klaas Worp in *O.Bankes*, pp. 61–62. For Trajan's titulature in general, see Bureth 1964, pp. 46–54.

[. . . . .]μ̣ε̣ν̣α .[. . . .]

- -

1 ἀντίγρ ϛ; l. συγγραφῆς || **11** l. δοκιμίου || **12** l. ὑέλινα

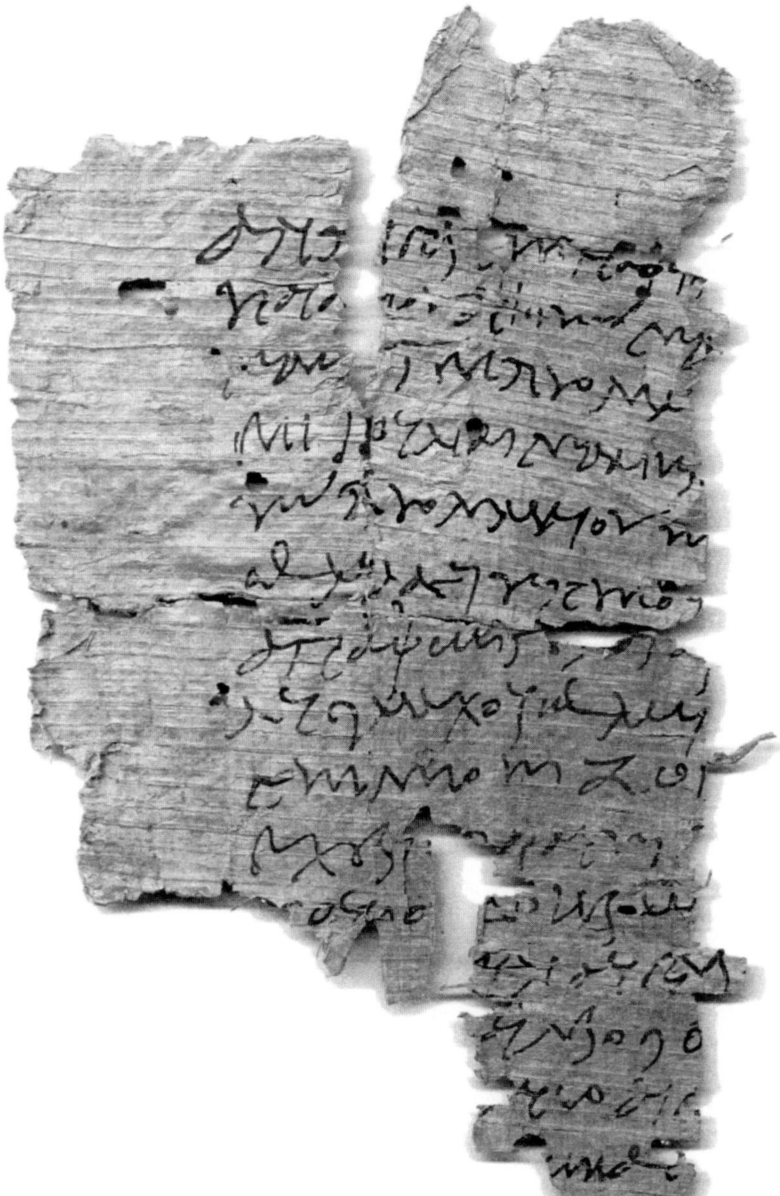

[94]

TRANSLATION

Copy of a contract. Year *x* of Imperator Caesar Nerva Traianus Optimus Augustus Germanicus Dacicus, the tenth of the month Neos Sebastos, in Ptolemais Euergetis of the Arsinoite nome, in the presence of Iulia Augusta. NN son of NN grandson of Ptolemaios alias NN, Persian of the *epigone*, about 42 years old, without distinguishing marks, acknowledges to his previous and still cohabiting wife without a written marriage contract, NN daughter of NN, granddaughter of Lysimachos, about 48 years old, that he received from her for her dowry, *x* quarters of acceptable gold... glass-gem rings, ... total the above-mentioned quarters?

COMMENTARY

1–2. On Trajan's titulature here and its implication for the date of this papyrus, see above, introd. with n. 1. I owe the reading of Ἀρίστου to Graham Claytor.

4. ἐπὶ Ἰουλίας Σεβαστῆς: "in the presence of Julia Augusta." The name of the empress was used in the marriage oath taken by the couple, probably before her statue. Other marriage contracts with the same expression come from the Arsinoite and Oxyrhynchite nomes: *P.Ups.Frid* 2, 1–2 (Tebtynis (?), 59/60); *BGU* I 252, 2–3 (Ptolemais Euergetis, 98 CE); *SB* XXIV 16256, 2 (Ptolemais Euergetis, 109 CE); *P.Oxy.* III 496, 1 (Oxyrhynchos, 127 CE); *SPP* XX 5 (Ptolemais Euergetis, 136 CE); *P.Stras.* IV 237, 4 (Ptolemais Euergetis, 142 CE); *CPR* VII 33, 1 (Provenance unknown, II CE); *SB* XXVIII 17046 (see Yiftach-Firanko 2003, p. 332, no. 2), (Oxyrhynchos, II CE). All the previous instances, except *P.Ups. Frid.* 2, of 59/60 CE, are dated to the first half of the second century CE. *P.Ups. Frid.* 2 has been considered interesting due to the fact that it comes from a village rather than the nome capital, which is the case in all the other instances from the Arsinoite (so Sijpesteijn 1996, p. 167, line 2 comm., and Yiftach-Firanko 2003, p. 332, no. 2 (= *SB* XXVIII 17046), line 1 comm. For the significance of this expression, see Wilcken 1909, and Sijpesteijn 1996, p. 167, line 2 comm. For the cult of deified Livia, associated with Juno (*Pronuba*) as the guardian of married life, see Grether 1946, esp. p. 242, and Flory 1984, esp. pp. 319–320. Other members of the Imperial Cult are also attested in the same context in Oxyrhynchos in the second half of the second century: *P.Oxy.* VI 905, 1, with *BL* VII p. 132, (170 CE): [ἐπὶ Ἀντωνί]ν̣ου καὶ Φαυστείνας Σεβαστῶν (cf. *BL* I 328: [ἐπὶ Μάρκου Ἀντωνί]νου, taken also by Yiftach-Firanko (2003, p. 332, no. 2, 1 comm.); *PSI Congr.* XX 10 (173 CE): ἐπὶ Φαυστείνης καὶ Ἰουλίας Σεβαστῶν.

5. τοῦ Πτολεμαίου το[ῦ καί: by reason of space this should be the paternal grandfather, who had a double name. After the double name might have stood a matronymic. But since a mother's name is not mentioned in the case of the wife or her guardian, the lacuna had Πέρσης τῆς ἐπιγονῆς. On this designation, see **91**, 5 comm.

6–7. τῇ συνού[σῃ . . . .] | ἀγράφως γ̣υ̣ναικί: the usual formula in marriage contracts is τῇ προούσῃ καὶ συνούσῃ αὐτῷ ἀγράφως γυναικί as, e.g., in *P.Mil.Vogl.* II 71, 3–4 (Ptolemais Euergetis, 172–175 CE). Yiftach-Firanko (2003, p. 95) translates προούσῃ καὶ συνούσῃ γυνή as "previous and still cohabiting wife." One finds the same formula, but with the order of the participles reversed, in the context of marriage in *P.Wisc.* I 36, 16 (Theadelphia, 147 CE), where the scribe added καὶ προούσῃ above the line. The same also applies to *BGU* I 183, 29 (Soknopaiou Nesos, 85 CE), which should be transcribed συνούσης καὶ προ{ο̣υ̣}ούσης rather than the editor's συνούσης καὶ προ<γα>μ̣ο̣ύσης.[1] The restoration of the present line as τῇ συνού[σῃ καὶ προούσῃ αὐτῷ], however, is too short for the lacuna. Furthermore, since this reverse order of the participles was doubtless the result of miscopying, it could well be that the present scribe, after writing συνού̣[σῃ, noticed that he had mistakenly anticipated the second participle and added the correct phrase immediately afterwards. The reconstruction [[τῇ συνού̣[σῃ]] τῇ προούσῃ καὶ συνούσῃ αὐτῷ] | ἀγράφως would be in keeping with the standard formula and would sufficiently fill the gap.

7. ἀγράφως: for the unwritten marriage, see Yiftach-Firanko 2003, pp. 81–103. Documents which record the transformation of ἄγραφος γάμος into ἔγγραφος are listed in Wolff 1939, p. 58, n. 205. For a list of pertinent documents published after Wolff's work, see *P.Hamb.* III 220, introd.

10. ἔχειν παρ'αὐτῆς̣ [ἐφ' ἑαυτῇ φερνὴν ....]: no supplement can be offered with certainty. Likely an amount of money as, e.g., in *P.Stras.* VII 668, 3–5 (Provenance unknown, II CE): ἐφ' ἑ̣α̣υ̣τ̣[ῇ] φερνὴν ἀργ[(υρίου) δρ]αχμὰς ἑκατὸν καὶ ἐν παραφέρ[νο]ι̣ς χρυσίου κοινοῦ.

11. χρυσοῦ δοκειμε̣[ίου τετάρτας: the τετάρτη, i.e. one sixteenth of the μναιαῖον, is a well-attested weight that was used exclusively for gold; see *P.Graux* II 10, 7–8 comm., and Russo 1999, p. 3. For acceptable gold and various types of gold, see Russo 1999, pp. 252–256.

12. δακ]τ̣ύλια ὑέλειν̣[α: for the interchange of ὑελ- and ὑαλ-, see Gignac 1981, p. 282. Although glass jewelry was fairly common in Egypt, none is attested in documentary papyri so far. It is, however, attested in a glossary Περὶ χρυσέων κοσμημάτων = *P.Scholl* 4, 43, where it is a synonym for the Latin *vitreus*, see the commentary in *P.Scholl*, p. 158. Cf. also the melted stone (χυτός λίθος), i.e. glass, in *P.Oxy.* XII 1449, 20, 24; XLIX 3473, 12; Russo 1999, p. 69, n. 27. For various kinds of rings, see Russo 1999, pp. 163–187; Ogden 1990, pp. 104–142.

1. The fact that προγαμέω is attested in no other papyrus raises doubts about the reading. A look at the online image—http://www.papyrology.uw.edu.pl/papyri/pberlin6867r.jpg—makes the reading of dittographic προ{ο̣υ̣}ούσης.

95. Receipt for Repayment of a Loan (from the Dossier of Zeuxis)

P.Fouad inv. 126 | w 9.5 × h 16.7 cm | 125/126 CE
Tebtynis

The recto of this fragment preserves the lower left of a document written along the fibers with margins of ca. 2 cm visible to the left of the text and below it. The papyrus was vertically folded four times. The back contains a docket, written along the fibers, perpendicular to the text on the recto. It is written about 4 cm below the upper edge of the verso, which corresponds with the right edge of the recto. The docket is badly damaged but seems to be written in a hand different from that on recto.

The present text is part of the dossier of the family of Zeuxis son of Dios, an Alexandrian citizen of the Sosikosmian tribe and the Althaean deme. The family is known from other published documents in the Fouad collection between 125 and 148 CE. The dossier and the members of the family have long been recognized by van Minnen (1993, pp. 118–119). According to the family tree produced by van Minnen, three members of the family are identified: two brothers Dios (born ca. 106 CE) and Tyrannos (born ca. 108 CE) and a sister Ptolemais (if the supplement of line 8 is right, Ptolemais is 42 years old, which means that she was born ca. 84 CE, and therefore older than Dios; cf. line 8 comm. below). For an overview of this dossier see Elmaghrabi 2020.

Here, Tyrannos together with his elder sister Ptolemais issues a receipt to Thaisarion daughter of Didymos for the partial repayment of a loan.

It is possible to date the present text on the basis of the fact that the same Tyrannos is mentioned as being 18 years old in *P.Fouad* 51 of 126 CE. Since he has the same age in the present document, it should likewise be dated to 125–126 CE (see lines 1–2 comm.).

\- -
→ [. . . . . . .].[. . . . .]
[. . . . . . .]φ[. . . . .]
[. . ὁ]μ̣[ο]λ(ογοῦσι) Τ̣ύ̣[ραννος ὁ καὶ Ἰσίδωρος]
Ζεύξιδος Σωσ̣ι[κό]σ̣[μ(ειος) ὁ καὶ Ἀλθ(αιεὺς) ὡς]
ἐτῶν δέκ̣[α ὀ]κτὼ [οὐλὴ μετώπῳ ἐξ ἀ-]
ριστερῶν ὑπὸ τρί[χα καὶ ἡ τούτου]
ὁμοπάτριος καὶ ὁ[μομήτριος ἀδελ-]
φὴ Πτ̣ο̣λεμα<ῒς> [[μ]] ὡ̣ς̣ ἐ̣τῶ[ν τεσσαράκοντα]
δύο ἄσημος μετ̣[ὰ κυρίου τοῦ προ-]
γεγραμμένου ἀδ̣[ελφοῦ Τυράννου]
Θαισαρίῳ Διδύμ[ου τοῦ . .] . . [. . . ε-]
ως ὡς ἐτῶν τ̣ρ̣ι̣ά̣κ̣ο̣ν̣τ̣α̣ ἑπ[τὰ οὐ-]
λὴ μετώπῳ μέσῳ μετὰ κυρ[ίου τοῦ]
ἑαυ̣τ̣[ῆ]ς ἀνδ̣ρ̣ὸς Ἐκύσε[ως τοῦ Πα-]

ποντῶτος ὡ̣ς ἐτ[ῶν τεσσαράκον-]
τα πέντε οὐλὴ̣ [. . . . . ἀπ-]
έχειν παρ' α̣ὐ̣τ̣ῆ̣ς [. . . . .]
ἀργυρίου δραχμ̣[ὰς διακοσίας (?) εἴ-]
κοσι ἓξ ἀπὸ δ[ραχμῶν - - -, ὧν ὤφει-]
λεν ἑ̣α̣υτοῖ̣ς̣ .̣ [. . . . . , κατὰ]
μηδὲν \`δὲ´ αὐτῷ̣[ν ἐλαττουμένων]
ὑπ[ὲρ] ἧς ἔχ[ουσι . . . .]

verso:

→ (*m.* 2) ἀ[ποχὴ] Πτολεμαΐ(δος) καὶ Τυράννου.

3 ο]μ[ο]$^{\lambda}$

[95 recto]

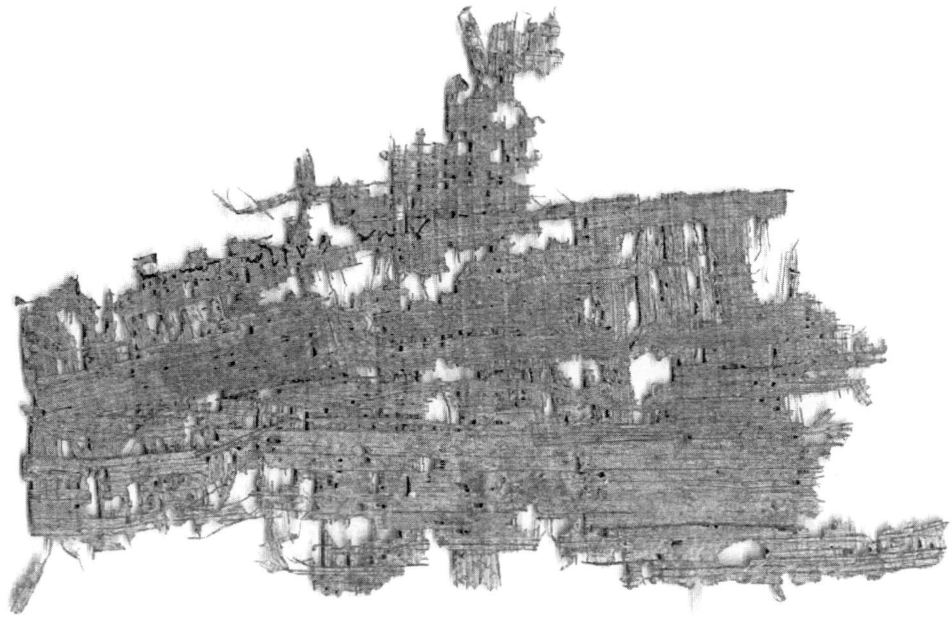

[95 verso]

TRANSLATION

... Tyrannos alias Isidoros son of Zeuxis, of the Sosikosmian tribe and the Althaean deme, about eighteen years old, with a scar on the left side of his forehead beneath the hair, and his sister by the same father and mother, Ptolemais, about forty two years old, without identification marks, acting with her guardian the aforementioned brother Tyrannos, acknowledge to Thaisarion daughter of Didymos son of NN about thirty seven years old, with a scar in the middle of her forehead, with her husband Ekysis son of Papontos, about forty (?) five years old, as her guardian, that they have received from her two hundred (?) twenty six silver drachmas from the... drachmas which she owes them... They shall suffer no loss with regard to the loan contract which they have (?)...

Verso: Receipt of Ptolemais and Tyrannos.

COMMENTARY

1–2. These lines should date the papyrus, presumably as follows: ἔτους δεκάτου (or ι) Αὐτοκράτορος Καίσαρος Τραιανοῦ Ἁδριανοῦ Σεβαστοῦ. The *phi* is doubtless part of a month name. One cannot exclude Φ[αωφι, Φ[αμενωθ or Φ[αρμουθι, but Φαω]φ[ι and Ἐπει]φ are more likely given the amount of space needed for the locality formula ἐν Τεβ(τύνει) τῆς Πολ(έμωνος) μερ(ίδος) τοῦ Ἀρσ(ινοΐτου) νομ(οῦ). The date, then, is probably 28 September – 27 October 125 CE/ 25 June – 24 July 126 CE.

3. For the *homologia* form in repayment of loan documents see *P. Yale* I 63, introduction.

3–5. Τ̣ύ̣[ραννος ὁ καὶ Ἰσίδωρος] | Ζεύξιδος Σωσ̣ι[κό]σ̣[μει(ος) ὁ καὶ Ἀλθ(αιεὺς) ὡς] | ἐτῶν δέκ̣[α ὀ]κτὼ [οὐλὴ μετώπῳ ἐξ ἀ]|ριστερῶν ὑπὸ τρί[χα: cf. *P.Fouad* 51, 7–9 (Tebtynis, 126 CE): Τύραννος ὁ καὶ Ἰσίδωρος ὡς ἐτῶν δέκα ὀκτώ, οὐλὴ μετώπῳ ἐξ ἀρ[ιστ]ερῶν ὑπὸ τρίχα.

8. Πτ̣ο̣λεμα<ΐς> [[μ̣]] ὡ̣ς̣ ἐ̣τῶ[ν: the name of the sister on the verso appears to be Πτολεμαί(δος) and *P.Fouad* 55, 1 has Πτολεμαείς. It could also be that Πτολεμαΐς was known as Πτολέμα and that emendation is not necessary. The first letter in the difficult ὡ̣ς̣ is involved in a correction, perhaps the scribe had started to write μετά and realised that he had forgotten the age. The small and cramped first letter of ἐ̣τῶ[ν is likewise difficult.
The supplement τεσσαράκοντα exactly fits the lacuna, but τριάκοντα would not be too short at the end of line. In both cases Ptolemais, being born in 84 or 94 CE, should have been the eldest of Zeuxis's children (Dios was born 105/6 CE and Tyrannos in 107/8 CE). Either 12 or 22 years of age-gap is quite a lot between siblings from same mother. For birth intervals see Bagnall, Frier 1994, p. 150, n. 52.

13–16. τοῦ] | ἑαυ̣τ̣[ῆ]ς ἀνδ̣ρ̣ὸς Ἐκύσε[ως τοῦ Πα]|ποντῶτος ὡς ἐτ[ῶν τεσσαράκον]|τα πέντε: the restoration of τεσσαράκον]|τα fills the available space and establishes a very likely eight-year difference between the ages of the husband and the wife. For 7.5 years as the mean age gap between husband and wife in the census returns, see Bagnall, Frier 1994, p. 118.

16–17. ἀπ]|έχειν παρ᾽ α̣ὐτ̣ῆ̣ς [. . . . .] | ἀργυρίου δραχμ̣[άς: the restoration of [τοὺς ὁμολογοῦντας] is not necessarily too long nor is [διὰ χειρός] or [Θαϊσαρίου] necessarily too short.

19–20. ἀπὸ δ[ραχμῶν - - -, ὧν ὤφει]|λεν ἑ̣αυτοῖ̣ς̣ . [. . . . . : the amount of the original debt will have been written as one or more numeral letters. One might also consider ἀπὸ δ[ανείου οὗ etc., in which case the amount should be included in line 20.

22. ὑπ[ὲρ] ἧς ἔχ[ουσι . . . .]: one might consider, for example, ὑπὲρ ἧς ἔχ[ουσι δανείου συγγραφῆς], see *P.Mich.* V 341, 7–9 (Tebtynis, before 47 CE): κατὰ μηδὲν τῶν τῆς Ἡρακλέας γονέων Διδύμου τοῦ Μάρωνος καὶ Ῥοδοῦτος τῆς Ἡρακλήας ἁπλῶς ἐλ̣αττουμένου ὑπὲρ ἧς ἔχουσι τῆς Ἡρακλέας κατὰ πατρικῶν καὶ μητρικῶν ἐπὶ τοῦ αὐτοῦ δευτέρου ἔτους Τιβερίου Κλαυδίου Καίσαρος Σεβαστοῦ Γερμανικοῦ Αὐτοκράτορος μηνὶ vac. διὰ τοῦ αὐτοῦ γραφείου ἐκστάσεως. Cf. also *P.Stras.* VII 646, 11 (Arsinoite, 117–138 CE): - - - κατὰ μηδ]ὲ̣ν τῆς Σωτ̣αροῦτος τ̣ῆ̣[ς κα]ὶ Πασιαν̣ῆ̣ς ἐλα[τ]τουμένη̣[ς ὑπ]ὲρ ἧς ἔχει τη[- - - . This clause, which appears only in the Roman period, is intended to reserve further claims for the creditor against the debtor or a co-debtor; see Hage 1970, and Rupprecht 1971, p. 18.

96. Complaint about a Physical Assault

P.Fouad inv. 72 — w 09 × h 22 cm — 13.2.157 CE
Bakchias, Arsinoite

The papyrus is broken away on its right side, badly worm-eaten in some places, but is otherwise nearly complete (margins: upper 1.5 cm, left 2 cm, lower 2 cm). The writing runs along the fibers on the recto. The back is blank.

The text, a complaint about a physical assault written in the form of a *hypomnema*, is addressed to Theodoros, *strategos* of the Arsinoite nome, for the meris of Herakleides, and is dated to the 19th of Mecheir in the 2nd year of Antoninus (157 CE). It follows the usual structure: (1) date and place; (2) mention of the individuals involved; (3) description of the nature of the injury; and (4) request to summon the culprit(s). Since the subscription of the petitioner is left out, what we have is probably a copy.

The present complaint by a certain Pnepheros, whose father's name is not preserved, concerns violence done against his brother Dionysios. His injuries were so severe that they resulted in his being bed-ridden and in danger of his life. This is doubtless the reasons that his brother Pnepheros filed the complaint.

The assault took place while the victim was visiting a temple "near" his home village πρὸς τῇ κώμῃ. Strangely, the petitioner does not specify which temple it is (see comm. on lines 7–8, 9). What the victim was doing in the temple is described in the damaged area in lines 7–8, probably by a single participle (see comm.). Leaving aside official violence against persons who took asylum in temples, assaults by private individuals is attested in a few other papyri. From the Ptolemaic period, *UPZ* I 119 (a report over interrogation, Memphis, 156 BCE) shows some sort of violence within the vicinity of the temple. In *P.Stras.* II 91 (Arsinoite, 87? BCE) violence was committed against temple personnel on duty and in *P.Tebt.* III/1 797 a priest was attacked and robbed, whilst actually engaged in religious rites. In *P.Tebt.* I 39 (114 BCE) the two parties are priests, but the victim is acting in his capacity as contractor for the distribution of and the tax upon oil, the incident however took place in a house located in the temple. From the Roman period, we have some examples, mainly from Soknopaiou Nesos, a village with high priestly presence, showing that priests were subject to some sort of violence, and who drafted petitions; cf. e.g. *P.Louvre* I 1 (3 CE), *SB* I 5235 (14 CE) and *BGU* I 36 = *M.Chr.* 125 (98–117 CE) of which *BGU* II 436 is a duplicate. None of these incidents, however, actually took place in the temple, although the incident recorded in *SB* VI 9238, 6–8 seems to have taken place in the vicinity of a temple: ἡμῶν, κύριε, ἀναλυόντ[ων] ἀπὸ τοῦ ἱερ[ο]ῦ, ἐπῆλθαν ἡμῖν [κα]κοῦρ[γοι] "*Nous revenions, Monsieur, du temple (ou du sacrifice)*" (Rémondon in the ed. princ.).The new papyrus is the first attestation for an action of violence taking place in a temple; unfortunately the circumstances that led to the violence are not stated in the petition.

The person who wrote the present text is in all likelihood the same as the one who wrote *PSI* XV 1526 of 160 CE, a petition written three years later, also in Bakchias. The handwritings of the two are very similar, the main difference being that *PSI* 1526 was written with a thicker pen (photo available at http://www.psi-online.it/documents/psi;15;1526). There is also a number of idiosyncrasies common to both; see comments on lines 12 οὐκ ὀλίγας, 21 ἀκθῆναι for ἀχθῆναι, 22–23 τύχω διὰ τῆς σῆς βοηθ[εί]ας.

→ [Θε]ο̣δώρῳ στρ̣(ατηγῷ) Ἀρσι̣(νοΐτου) Ἡ̣[ρακλ(είδου)]
μερίδος.
[παρὰ Π]ν̣εφερῶτος τοῦ [̣ ̣ ̣ ̣]
[̣ ̣ ̣]ς̣ τῶν ἀπ̣[ὸ] κ̣ώμ̣[ης]
[Βακ]χ̣ιάδος. τῇ [ι ̣] τ̣οῦ ὄ̣[ντος]
[μην]ὸς Μεχ̣ε̣[ὶρ το]ῦ ἀδελ-
[φοῦ] μ̣ου Δι[ον]υ̣σ̣ίου ̣[̣]
̣ν̣[̣ ̣ ̣]υ̣ντος ἐν ἱερῷ [τῷ]
πρ[ὸς] τῇ κώμῃ, ἐπῆλθ[εν αὐ-]
τῷ ̣ ̣[̣]ίθης Πετεσο[ύχου]
μετ̣' [ἄ]λ̣λων καὶ ἐπήν[εγκε]
αὐτ[ῷ] πληγὰ̣ς ο̣ὐ̣χ̣ ὀλ[ίγα]ς̣
κατὰ [μ]ὲ̣ν τῆς κ̣εφαλῆ̣ς κ̣α̣[ὶ]
τοῦ μ̣ηροῦ κ̣[αὶ ὅ]λου̣ [τοῦ σώ-]
ματ̣ο̣[ς], ὥστε αὐτὸ[ν τραυ-]
μ̣ατισθῆναι τραυμα[̣ ̣ ̣ ̣ ̣]
τ̣α̣[ι]ς <καὶ> κλινήρην αὐτὸν [γε-]
νέσθαι καὶ κινδυν̣[εύειν]
τῷ ζῆν. ἀξιῶ καταχω-
ρισθῆναι τόδε τὸ ὑπόμ<ν>η-
μα καὶ ἀκθῆναι αὐτὸν ἐπί σε̣
ὅ[πω]ς τύχῳ διὰ τῆς σῆς
βοηθ[εί]ας. διευτύχει.
vac.
(ἔτους) κ̅ Ἀντωνείνου Καίσαρος
τοῦ κυρί[ο]υ Μεχ(εὶρ) ιθ̅.

1 στρ/ || **8** ϊερω || **12** l. οὐκ || **17** l. κλινήρη || **20** ϋπομνημα || **21** l. ἀχθῆναι || **25** με^{χ}: ex μεθ corr.

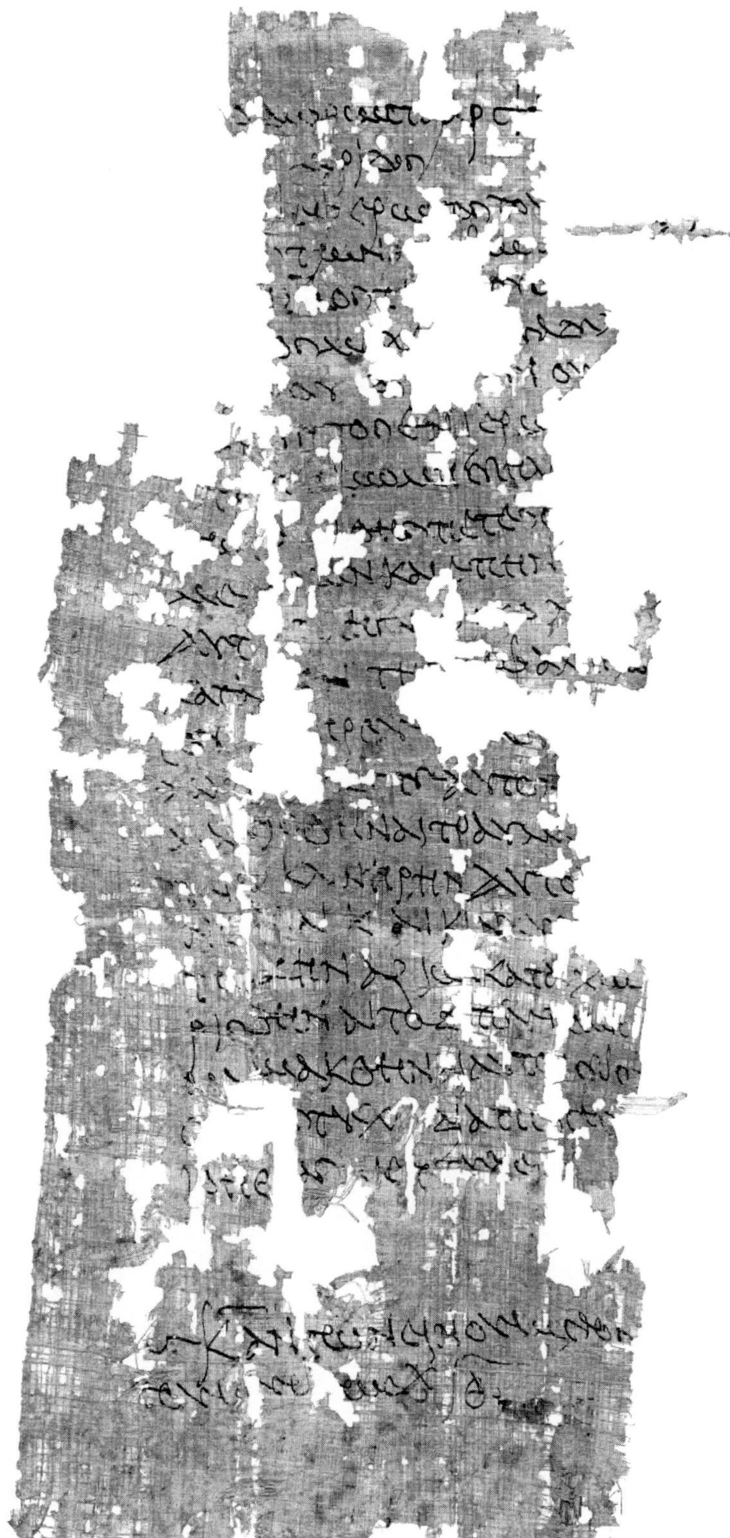

[96]

TRANSLATION

To Theodoros, *strategos* of the Arsinoite, for the meris of Herakleides. From Pnepheros son of NN, from the village of Bakchias, on the 11th–18th of the current month Mecheir, while my brother Dionysios was… in the temple at the village, [Horbithes?] son of Petesouchos with others attacked him and struck no few blows on his head and thigh and entire body, so that he was wounded… and is bedridden and in danger of his life. I request that this complaint be registered and that he be brought before you, in order that we may receive through you help. Farewell. Year 20 of Antoninus Caesar the Lord, Mecheir 19.

COMMENTARY

1. Theodoros was the *strategos* of the Arsinoite nome in the meris of Herakleides, he is attested between February/March 156 (*BGU* XIII 2216) and 14 February 159 (*P.Lond.* II 376). He is addressed in *CPR* XV 21; *P.Lips.* 122; *SB* XII 11105; *P.Münch.* III/1 74; *P.Cair.Mich.* II 17. See Whitehorne 2006, p. 20. For petitions in general, see Kelly 2011. For the competence of the strategos and other officials in different kinds of petitions see Mascellari 2021, pp. 253–306 especially pp. 253–276 and 611–958 *passim*.

5. [Βακχ]ιάδος: there are only a few possibilities for village names that end in -ιας in the Herakleides meris: Hephaistias, Ammonias and Bakchias. The last of these is the most probable one for reason of space at the beginning of this line (c. 3 letters); see also introd. A raised horizontal stroke appears above the now damaged letters αδ; perhaps the scribe was about to abbreviate the word but changed his mind.
τῇ [ι .] τ̣οῦ ὄ̣[ντος]: there survives the extreme end of the raised horizontal line that marked the numeral-letters. That there were two numeral-letters is suggested by the space as well as by the fact that the petition was submitted on the 19th. Expected is a day from the 11th to the 18th. In cases of violent assault, petitions were usually submitted only a few days after the incident in question and occasionally the very day of the assault. On the amount of time between the date of an offence and that on which it was reported, see Kelly 2011, pp. 271–274.

6–7. το]ῦ ἀδελ|[φοῦ] μ̣ου Δι[ον]υ̣σ̣ίου: Kelly (2011, p. 221) lists 29 petitions submitted by one family member on behalf of another. Four of them are submitted by a brother of the victim: *P.Harr.* II 192 (Provenance unknown, 167 CE), *P.Tebt.* II 304 (Tebtynis, 168 CE), *P.Princ.* II 29 (Philadelphia, 258 CE) and *SB* XX 14229 (Oxyrhynchite, 259 CE).

7–8. [.]| . ν̣[.]υν̣τος: a present participle is expected here, describing what the victim was doing in the temple when the assault took place. The first letter in line 8 might be an alpha. H. Cuvigny proposes ἐ̣[π]-|α̣ν̣[τλο]ῦντος; Dionysios may have been occupied irrigating the garden of the temple when he was assaulted.
It is noteworthy that the scribe did not identify the temple, cf. the same situation "the temple that is in the village Bakchias" in *P.Bacch.* 19, 2–5 (171 CE): παρὰ [Πε]τεύριος Πετεύριος καὶ Σισόιτος [Ὀρ]σ̣ενούφεως καὶ τῶν λοιπῶν ἱε[ρ]έ̣ων ἱεροῦ τοῦ ὄ̣ντος ἐν κώμῃ Βακχιάδι.

BGU XIII 2215 (113/114 CE) attests to the existence of two temples in the village: Βακχιάδος ἱερὰ β Σοκνεβρ̣έσιος [καὶ Σο]κ̣ανεβκενέ̣ως καὶ τῶν συννάων θε̣ῶν. Recent archaeological research conducted at Bakchias has so far confirmed that two adjacent *temene* were active in the Roman period, dedicated to Soknobraisis and Soknobkonneus, a pair of minor local crocodile gods (emanations of the great crocodile god Sobek-Souchos), see Buzi, Giorgi 2020, pp. 38–54. *P.Bacch.* 1 (116 CE) and 2 (171 CE) attest both of these gods in wording that suggests they each had their own temple (see *P.Bacch.*, pp. 182–186), but perhaps these two temples were considered as one entity both here and in *P.Bacch.* 19. Other minor temples within the village are also attested such as e.g. the temple of Ammon in *P.Lund.* IV 9, 17 (164/165 CE) and the temple of Aphrodite in *SB* VI 9321, 9 (II CE).

9. πρὸς τῇ κώμῃ: I owe this reading to Benoît Laudenbach. The use of πρὸς τῇ κώμῃ instead of the usual ἐν τῇ κώμῃ is noteworthy. It is possible that the scribe did not mean that the temple is located near the village, he perhaps considered the sanctuary as a distinct area, cf. the description of the location of the Sarapeum at Oxyrhynchos in *SB* VIII 9824, 5 (31 CE) and *P.Oxy.* I 99, 6, 16 (55 CE).

10. Perhaps Ὡ̣ρ[β]ίθης. The name Horbithes is attested only in ostraca from Narmouthis (II/III CE), where it is a patronymic of a certain Tryphon, cf. *O.Lund* 25, 6; *P.Narm.* I 116, 2; 120, 2; 132, 15. The name would appear here for the first time in the nominative (cf. TM_Nam ID 29193 and *P.Narm.* I, index III s.n.).

12. οὐκ ὀλίγας: more commonly a comparative or superlative form of πολύς modifies the word for blows in this context. The exact expression, ἐπήνεγκε μοι πληγὰς οὐκ ὀλίγας, was used in *P.Stras.* IV 241, 11–12 (II CE) which belongs to a group of papyri from Bakchias according to its inventory number (see *P.Stras.* IV p. 89), cf. also *PSI* XV 1526, 12–14 (Bakchias, 160 CE), likely written by the same scribe, ὅθεν οὐχ (l. οὐκ) ὀλείγον (l. ὀλίγον) βλά[βο]ς ἐπηκολουθηκέναι ε̣[ἰ]ά̣θη. In the latter, the expression is used to describe the damage (βλάβος) incurred from an act of violence, not from the blows; cf. Mascellari 2021, pp. 495–498, with many examples for the use of this expression.

13. κατὰ [μ]ὲ̣ν τῆς κ̣εφαλῆ̣ς̣: for the head wounds as a result of violence, cf. *P.Oxy.* XVI 1885, 9 (Oxyrhynchos 509 CE); *P.Sarap.* 1, 14 (Hermopolite, 125 CE). For wounds as a result of violence more generally, see Bryen 2008, pp. 98–99 (in petitions), and p. 101 (in medical reports).

14–15. ὅλου̣ [τοῦ σώ]|ματο̣[ς]: there is hardly enough space for the article. Cf. *PSI* IV 313, 11 (III/IV CE), and the variant expression εἰς πᾶν μέρος τοῦ σώματος in e.g. *P.Ryl.* II 124, 24–26 (Euhemeria, I CE), 145, 14 (Euhemeria, 38 CE), and *BGU* XX 2870, 9–10 (Provenance unknown, I CE).

15–17. The passage is problematic, and I cannot offer any plausible restoration. Instead of assuming a mistake *iuxta lacunam*, i.e. [τραυ-]μ̣ατισθῆναι {τραυμα[τισθῆ]|ν̣α̣ι̣}, a *figura etymologica*, i.e. [τραυ-] | ματισθῆναι τραύμα[σι, would be more plausible. The traces at the beginning of line 17 is perhaps τ̣α̣ι̣ rather than ν̣α̣ι̣, followed by traces of perhaps one or two other letters that I can not identify, the trace of the second of which resmbles the left loop of a upsilon, but this is far from certain. Did the scribe erroneously write πλείσταις for πλείστοις? πληγαῖς πλείσταις is frequently attested in similar petitions, and confusion may be the reason for such an error. In this case one should type τραύμα[σι πλείσ-]|ṭα̣[ι]ς (l. πλείστοις). Although it is possible to read ṭα̣[ι]ς at the beginning of line 17, the available space for the lacuna at the end of line 16 can hardly accommodate more than five letters (cf. ἐπί σε̣ at the end of line 21), and the second αὐτόν would be superfluous. In addition, καί is impossible to be read anywhere before κλινήρην; but it is sometimes written in *Verschleifung* as at the end of line 13 and in line 21, otherwise we should assume asyndeton. In parallels we usually find the confined to bed phrase connected with the referential conjunction ἐκ τούτου in this place. see e.g. *W.Chr.* 268=*BGU* II 515, 21–22 (Arsinoite, 193 CE): [διὸ ἐκ τ]ούτου τε κλει-|[νήρου]ς (l. κλι|[νήρου]ς) α[ὐτῆς γ]ενομένης and *BGU* I 45, 13–15 (Arsinoite, 203 CE): πληγαῖς πλείσταις αὐτὸν | ἤκισαν καὶ ἐκ τούτου κλεινήρη (l. κλινήρη) | γεγονέναι. Another possiblity is to restore τραύμα[σι, τρι]|ṭα̣ῖ[ο]ṿ κλινήρην etc., i.e. he has been bedridden for three days. While this restoration may explain the insertion of αὐτόν, it will also require assuming asyndeton.

18–19. κινδυṿ[εύειν] | τῷ ζῆν: the theme of being in danger of losing one's life is a common in petitions dealing with assault, see Mascellari 2021, pp. 428–431, and Bryen 2008, pp. 98–99, n. 94.

19–21. ἀξιῶ καταχω-|ρισθῆναι τόδε τὸ ὑπόμν[η-]|μα: the usual formula is ἐν καταχωρισμῷ γενέσθαι, an expression usually used when the culprits are unknown; cf. *P.Oxy.* L 3561, 16–17 (Arsinoite, c. 165 CE): ἀξιῶ ἐν κατα[χωρι]σ̣μ̣ῷ γενέσθαι̣ παρὰ σοὶ τό̣δε. In *P.Fay.* 108, 25–29 (Ptolemais Euergetis, 169 or 170 CE), the purpose of the registration is that when the culprits are discovered the petitioners may bring a charge against them (cf. also *CPR* XV 7, 8 comm.; 8, 19–21 comm., and *P.Fouad* 29, 12 comm.). This explanation, however, does not apply to the present case. In many petitions, usually addressed to the *strategos*, the petitioner asks that his petition be archived in order to maintain his right (*logos*), perhaps as evidence at a following trial; see Kelly 2011, pp. 198–199, n. 156; Mascellari 2021, pp. 587–610.

21. ἀκθῆναι: *PSI* XV 1526, 14–15 (Bakchias, 160 CE) gave ἀχθῆ|ṿα̣ι, but the photo suggests rather ἀκθῆ|ṿα̣ι, a minor detail suggesting that both documents were written by the same writer.

22–23. ὅ[πω]ς τύχω διὰ τῆς σῆς | β̣ο̣ηθ[εί]ας: the same curious phrasing occurs in *PSI* XV 1526, 16, written by the same scribe (see introd., pp. 41–42). For an explanation of the superfluous διά, see Mascellari 2021, p. 675, n. 53 and p. 966, n. 15.

23. διευτύχει: for διευτύχει in closing farewell in petitions see Mascellari 2018, pp. 294–305. According to Mascellari διευτύχει became dominant after 117 CE.

23–24. Between these two lines is a blank space of ca. 2 cm. Probably a signed copy was sent to the *strategos*, whereas the present unsigned copy was kept in the petitioner's papers, see Kelly 2011, pp. 70, 150–151.

97. Notification to the Property-Register Office (προσαγγελία)

P.Fouad Inv. 252 A w 11.3 × h 17.7 cm 13.10.160 CE
Lykopolis

Consisting of six at least partly joining fragments, **97** is almost complete, preserving parts of the left and lower margins. It is inscribed along the fibers on the recto. The back contains the first three letters of what appears to be the beginning of a docket written across the fibers.

The present text (and the duplicate **98**) is a notification of intent to sell a property dated to the 24th year of Antoninus Pius. It is a well-known type of document, usually referred to in the papyrological literature as a *prosangelia*. It is a prerequisite for drawing up a contract through the state notaries. The purpose of such notifications is to ensure that the property is registered under the name of the applicant and is free from all encumbrances according to the archives of immovable property (βιβλιοθήκη ἐγκτήσεων).[1] If these conditions were met, the keepers of the archives (βιβλιοφύλακες) communicated the pertinent information to the state notaries in an *epistalma*. Without this *epistalma* the notaries could not conclude a contract.[2] The *bibliophylakes* usually form a college of two, but it happens sometimes, as here, that a request or declaration is addressed to one only.

The prospective seller is Poous son of Panechates, grandson of Panechates. He addresses the notification to the keeper of the archives of immovable property of the Lykpolite nome. The property that is to be sold is the third of two arouras located in the southern fields of Lykopolis. Poous' sister Senpounsis, who shared with him the usufruct (καρπεία) of this property, had to give her consent (εὐδόκησις) to the sale.[3] She was entitled to this share of the usufruct for the length of time that her mother was alive according to a document made nine years earlier. The description of that document is lost in both **97** and **98** but it was probably a will or a division of inherited property. Other *prosangeliai* usually mention the name of the purchaser and the price. Their absence in **97** (and **98**) suggests that the main concern was to secure the sister's consent.

Appended to the text is the notification (*epistalma*) of Didymos alias Theon, identified as a former *bibliophylax*. He states that Poous has registered his third share of the two arouras together with the usufruct reserved for the sister. The purpose of this statement is obscured by the absence of an addressee or instructions. In addition, it is exceptional that in our document the *bibliophylax* is designated as a *former* one. The *bibliophylax*, however, is sometimes attested as having formerly held another office (gymnasiarch or *exegetes*). The fact that the first letters of βιβλιοφύλαξ were corrected from something else (which I have not been able to read) might be connected with this problem.

1. For the institution of the *Bibliotheke Enkteseon* (created about 72 CE), see Wolff 1978, pp. 48–51; Maresch 2002; Jördens/Yiftach-Firanko 2010; Alonso 2010.

2. On this so-called *epistalma*-system, see *Chrest.Mitt.* 2.1, pp. 97–103; von Woess, 1924, pp. 175–201; Wolff 1978, pp. 247–253. For a list of *prosangeliai*, see Harmon 1934, p. 171, n. 51. To this list may be added *BGU* XI 2092, *P.Heid.* IV 301 and the here edited **97** and **98**.

3. On εὐδόκησις in legal transactions involving joint heirs, see Wieacker 1931, esp. p. 411.

Apart from the absence of the *epistalma* and the omission of the reference to the duration of the καρπεία, **97** and **98** are almost identical (cf. 10–11 comm.), with hands 1, 2, 3 and 5 in **97** matching hands 1, 2, 3 and 4 of **98**. The different hands in both documents indicate that they were not copies. As **97** contains the *epistalma*, it appears that it was intended to be forwarded to the pertinent official, while **98** was kept in the archive of the *bibliophylakion*.

→ [(*m.* 5) . . . . . σεση(μείωμαι) (ἔτους) κδ Φαῶ]φι ιϛ.
[(*m.* 1) . . . . βιβλ(ιοφύλακι) ἐγ]κ̣τ̣(ήσεων) Λυκοπ(ολίτου).
vacat
[παρὰ Πωοῦτος Πανε]χ̣ά̣του τοῦ Πα̣[νεχ(άτου)]
[μητ(ρὸς) . . . . τῆς καὶ] Λυκαινίδος τ̣[ῶν]
[ἀπὸ Λ]ύκων πόλ(εως). βούλ(ομαι) π̣ω̣λ(ῆσαι) τὸ ὑπάρχ(ον) μο̣[ι]
[μέρος γ´] (ἀρουρῶν) β ἐν τοῖς ἀπὸ νότου πεδίοις [Λύκ(ων)]
[πόλ(εως) ϑ εἰς τὸ . .] . μο( ) ϛ´ ἀπὸ νότ(ου) κληρονόμ(ων) [Ἁρ-]
[οννώφριος ἐ]π̣ὶ τῶι εὐδοκ(εῖν) τὴν ἀδελ(φήν) μο̣υ Σεν-
[ποῦνσιν ἕν]εκα̣ οὗ ἔχει μέρους (ἡμίσους) καρ̣-
[πείας τοῦ μ]έρους γ [τ]ῶν (ἀρουρῶν) β ἐπ̣ὶ τὸν̣
[τῆς ζωῆς τῆ]ς μ̣η̣τρὸ[ς] χ̣ρόνον [ἀ]κολ(ούθως) τῆι
[. . . . .]χ( ) τ̣ο̣ῦ̣ ι[ε] (ἔτους) Ἀντωνίνο̣υ̣
Καίσ[α]ρο[ς] τ̣ο̣[ῦ κ]υρίου Φ̣α̣ῶ̣φι θ̅· διὸ [ἀνα-]
φέρω ὅπως ἐπιστείλῃ[ς] τῶι μνήμ(ονι) χ[ρημα-]
τίσαι μοι ὡς καθήκει. κα̣ὶ̣ ὀ̣μνύω τὴ̣[ν]
Αὐτοκράτορος Καίσαρος Τίτου Α̣ἰλίου Ἁδ[ριανοῦ]
Ἀντωνίνου Σεβαστο̣ῦ̣ Εὐσ̣εβοῦς τύχ̣[ην]
μηδενὶ ὑποκεῖσθα̣[ι.]—— (ἔτους) κ[δ]
Αὐτοκράτορος Καίσαρο[ς Τ]ί̣[το]υ̣ Αἰλί[ου]
Ἁδριανοῦ Ἀντωνίνου Σεβαστ[οῦ Εὐσεβοῦς]
Φαῶφι ιϛ. (*m.* 2) Πωοῦς Πανεχάτο̣υ ἐπιδέδωκα.
(*m.* 3) Σενποῦνσις Πανεχάτου μετ[ὰ] κ̣υρίου ἐμοῦ τ̣οῦ σ̣υ̣γ[γενοῦς]
Ὡρίωνος Εὐδαίμονος εὐδ[ο]κῶ ὡς πρόκειται.
(*m.* 4) Δίδυμος ὁ καὶ Θέων γενόμ(ενος) βιβλιοφύλα[ξ]
δηλῶ αὐτὸν ἀπογεγράφθαι τὸ μέρο(ς) γ τ̣[ῶν ἀρου-]
ρῶν δύο, τηρουμένης τῇ ἀδελφ`ῇ´ α̣[ὐτοῦ καρ-]
πείας, ἥτις εὐδοκήσει τῶι τῆς π⸢ράσ⸣[εως]
χρηματισμῶι. ἔτους τετάρτ(ου) καὶ εἰκο̣[στοῦ]
Ἀντωνίνου Καίσαρος τοῦ κυρίου, Φα̣ῶ̣[φι ιϛ (?).]

verso

↓ δ . . [.] . [

2 Λυκο$^{\pi}$ || **5** πο$^{\lambda}$ | βου$^{\lambda}$ | π̣ω̣$^{\lambda}$ | υπαρ$^{\chi}$ || **6** 𐅵 || **7** νο$^{\tau}$ | κληρονο$^{\mu}$ || **8** ευδο$^{\kappa}$ | αδε$^{\lambda}$ || **11** [α]κο$^{\lambda}$ || **12** L || **14** μνη$^{\mu}$ || **18** L || **24** γενο$^{\mu}$ || βιβλιοφ post corr. || **26** τῇ ἀδελφῇ: ex τῆς ἀδελφῆς corr. || **28** τεταρ$^{\tau}$

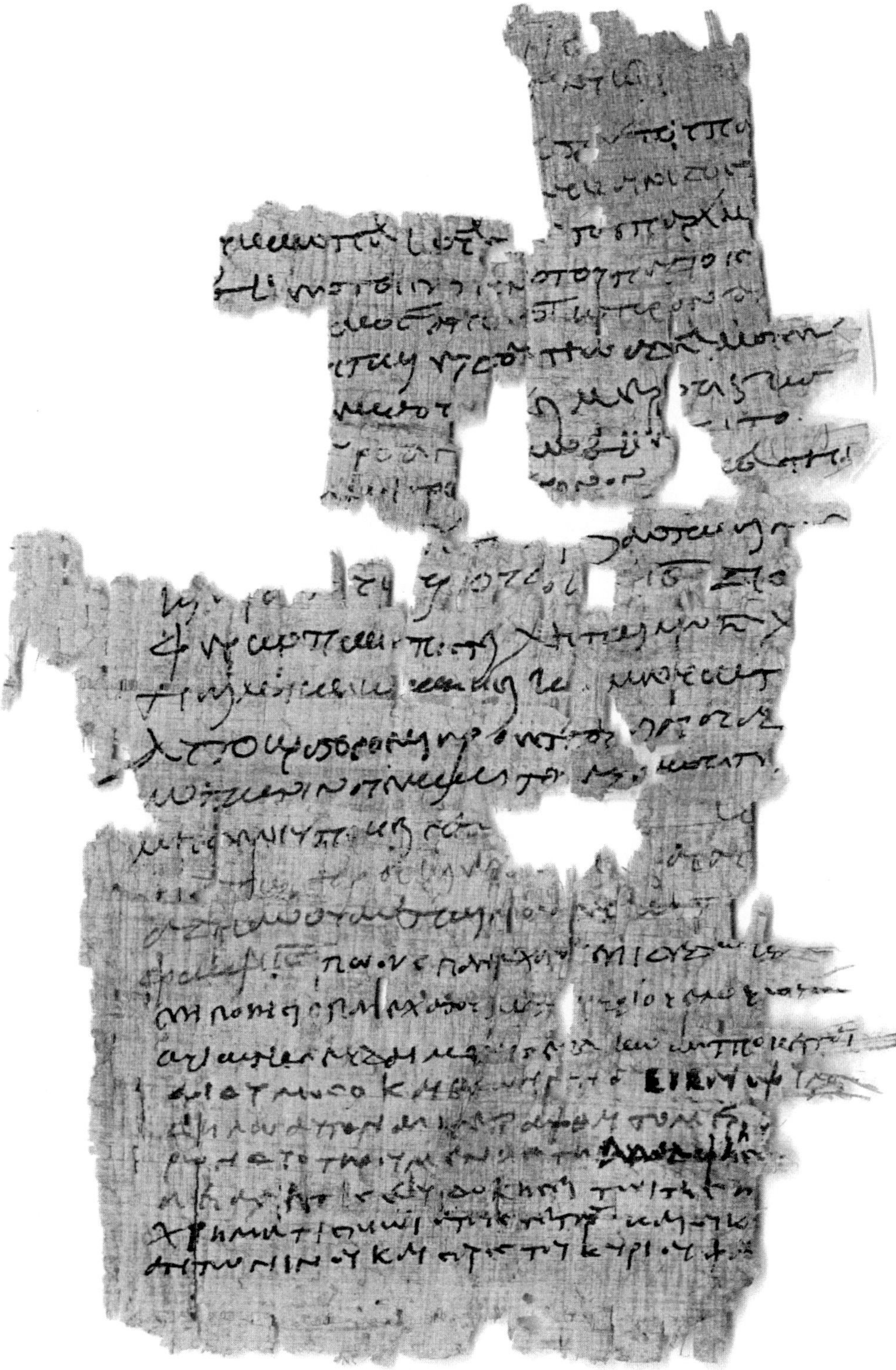

[97 recto]

[97 verso]

TRANSLATION

(5th hand) I NN have signed. Year 24, Phaophi 16. (1st hand) To NN keeper of the archives of landed property of the Lykopolite. From Poous son of Panechates, grandson of Panechates, his mother being NN alias Lykainis, from Lykopolis. I wish to sell the third part of two arouras that belongs to me in the southern fields of Lykopolis, 3/4... 1/6 to the south of the land of the heirs of Haronnophris, with the consent of my sister Senpounsis with regard to the half share of the usufruct which she holds for the period of our mother's lifetime in accordance with... the 15th year of Antoninus Caesar, the lord, in the month of Phaophi 9. I therefore give notice in order that you may send instructions to the registrar to issue the document for me, as it should be, and I swear by the fortune of Imperator Caesar Titus Aelius Hadrianus Antoninus Augustus Pius that (the piece of land) is not liable to anyone. Year 24 of Imperator Caesar Titus Aelius Hadrianus Antoninus Augustus Pius, Phaophi 16. (2nd hand) I Poous son of Panechates have submitted (this notification). (3rd hand) I Senpounsis daughter of Panechates, with my guardian, my relative Horion son of Eudaimon, give my approval as set forth above. (4th hand) I Didymos alias Theon, former *bibliophylax*, declare that he registered his third share of two arourai with the usufruct reserved to his sister, who will also give her consent to the deed of sale. The twenty-fourth year of Antoninus Caesar the lord, the 16th of Phaophi.

COMMENTARY

1. [. . . . . σεση(μείωμαι) (ἔτους) κδ Φαῶ]φι ιϛ: the name of the secretary is missing. The name of the secretary followed by the date is found in the upper margins (when preserved) of parallel documents; cf., e.g., *P.Lond.* II 299, 1–2 (Ptolemais Euergetis, 128 CE): Ἀπολ(λώνιος) σεση(μείωμαι) ιγ (ἔτους) Ἁδριανο(ῦ) τοῦ κυρίου Φαῶφι κθ.

2. [. . . . . βιβλ(ιοφύλακι) ἐγ]κ̣τ̣(ήσεων) Λυκοπ(ολίτου): we expect the name of the *bibliophylax* in the lacuna. The available space of ca. 8 letters is too small to accomodate Διδύμῳ τῷ καὶ Θέωνι. Possibly Διδύμῳ τῷ without the second name was written here. The same applies to the missing left side of **98**, 2. The restoration of Διδύμῳ τῷ would fill the space of ca 8 letters perfectly.

3. [Πωοῦτος Πανε]χ̣ά̣του τοῦ Πα̣[νεχ(άτου)]: cf. line 21; also **98**, 3 and 21. The otherwise unattested name Πωοῦς might be a variant spelling of rare Παωοῦς in *P.Oslo* III 195, 5 and 10 (Provenance unknown), cf. Ταπωοῦς in *SB* III 7057 2–3 (Panopolite). The father's name Πανεχάτης is common, cf. *Dem. Nam.*, pp. 382–383, and, for the occurrence of the name Πανεχάτης and other Egyptian names derived from the *ḫty*-demons in *P.Oxy.Census* see Bagnall 1998, p. 1096.

3–4. Πα̣[νεχ(άτου) | μη(τρός)]: the abbreviated words are to allow a space for the mother's name. μη(τρός) in **98**, 4 was perhaps written in full.

4. Λυκαινίδος: also in **98**, 4. This name has not been attested in the documentary papyri from Egypt till now. In Lykopolis it reflects that city's cult of the jackal god, *Wepwawet*, whom the Greeks generally regarded as a wolf. For other wolf-names in Lykopolis—Λύκος, Λυκαρίων, Λυκαριαίνη, Λυκόφορων, Λυκάων—mostly attested in *P.Oxy.Census* see Montevecchi 1998, esp. pp. 52–53; Montevecchi 2000; Bagnall 1998, p. 1095.

7. 𐅸 εἰς τὸ . .] . μο( ) ϛ´: reconstructed with **98**, 6–7. The sense is completely puzzling. The first and last pieces might be the fractions 3/4 and 1/6.

8–9. Σεν]|ποῦνσιν: restored with line 22; cf. **98**, 8–9, 21. This elsewhere unattested Egyptian woman's name is a variant of the occasionally attested Σενφούνσις/Σενπουόνσις/Σενπουῶνσις, meaning "daughter of Pounsis (wolf)." Like the aforementioned wolf-names, Pounsis (from Egyptian *wnš*) is characteristic of the Lykopolite. It is connected with the cult of Anubis, but distinct from it. Cf. Montevecchi, p. 52. For names derived from *wnš* attested in *P.Oxy.Census*, see Bagnall 1998, p. 1095.

9-10. I owe the reading of καρ|[πείας] to Dieter Hagedorn.

10–11. ἐπ̣ὶ τὸν̣ | [τῆς ζωῆς τῆ]ς μ̣η̣τρὸ[ς] χ̣ρόνον: omitted in **98**, 10.

11–12. [ἀ]κολ(ούθως) τῆι | [. . . . .]χ( ) τ . . ι[ε] (ἔτους) or (ἔτει): cf. **98**, 10–11 ἀκολ(ούθως) τῆι | [. . . . .]χ( ) ι̣ε (ἔτους) or (ἔτει). The reference is presumably to a legal arrangement that granted to the sister the *karpeia*. The will of a relative of the siblings seems probable. The first missing word in both passages, then, is probably διαθήκηι. Given the χ on the right edge of each of the lacunae, the will was probably that of the siblings' father or grandfather, both of whom were named Panechates. **97**, 12, then, probably had Πανε]χ(άτου) τ̣ο̣ῦ̣ or Πανε] χ̣ά̣τ̣ο̣υ̣, **98**, 11 probably had Πανε]χ(άτου). If these suggestions are on the right track, in the middle Panechates would have been identified as τοῦ πατρ(ός) or τοῦ πάπ(που). All this seems likely, but it is a tight fit, even if we assume that each word was abbreviated.

The immediately following date implies that the χ after the lacuna could, instead, stand for κε]χ(ρονισμένη̣) which of course fits the context (referring to the date on which the will (?) was drawn up). This is a well attested construction that is normally followed by εἰς or ἐπί. However, it is hard to see εἰς or ἐπί after the χ, and it could have been constructed with dative as in *P.Oxy.* XII 145, 221: κεχρονισμένη]ν τῷ ιε (ἔτει). This would render the phrase [διαθήκηι (?) κε]χ(ρονισμένη̣) τ̣ῷ̣ι̣ ι[ε] (ἔτει); the supplement however will then be a little shorter than expected (ca. 12 letters), and perhaps διαιρέσει should be supplemented.

14. ἐπιστείλη[ς]: **98** has the ἐπιστείλη̣ς. In **97** two fragments were placed too close to each other, giving the false impression that the writer omitted the sigma in ἐπιστείλη̣[ς]. The restoration of *M.Chr.* 202, 27 ἐὰν φα[ίνηται ἐπιστεί]λατε should be changed to ἐὰν φα[ίνηται ἐπισ]τ̣αλῆναι̣, see now *BOEP* 9.1, p. 3.

15–18. The oath is not an essential part of the *prosangelia*. As far as I am aware, the oath is only attested in *P.Oxy.* III 483 of 108 CE.

24. The *epistalma* is appended to the *prosangelia* within the official's subscription in *BGU* II 379, 20–25 (Karanis, 67 CE); *P.Oxy.* III 483, 32–37 (Oxyrhynchos, 108 CE); *P.Heid.* IV 301 I 13–20 (Herakleopolite, 192 CE); *SPP* XX 26, 49–56 (Herakleopolis, 224 CE). No *bibliophylax* of the Lykopolite is attested so far. For a list of *bibliophylakes*, see Sijpesteijn, Worp 1995, pp. 526–532.

26–27. τηρουμένης τῇ ἀδελφ`ῇ´ α̣[ὐτοῦ καρ]|πείας: cf. *P.Amh.* II 71, 13–14 (Hermopolis, 178/179 CE): ὧν ἡ [κ]αρπεία τοῦ (ἡμίσους) μέρους τετήρηται τῇ προγεγρ(αμμένῃ) μου μητρί.

27. π⌜ράσ⌝[εως]: this transcription is based on an old photo of the papyrus in the archives of the IFAO. The papyrus now has only π[.

98. Notification to the Property-Register Office (duplicate of 97)

P.Fouad Inv. 256 — w 8 × h 17 cm — 13.10.160 CE
Lykopolis

This is a duplicate of **97**. Inscribed along the fibers on the recto. The right, upper(?) and lower margins are partly extant. The back, to the extent that it is preserved, is blank. For the contents of this text, see **97**, introd. The commentary to **97** pertains to the present text as well. Only a few details found only in **98** are discussed in the commentary below.

→ [(*m.* 4) NN . . . . . . σεση(μείωμαι) (ἔτους) κδ] Φαῶφι ιϛ̅.
[(*m.* 1) NN . . . . βιβ]λ(ιοφύλακι) ἐνκτ(ήσεων) Λυκοπ̣(ολίτου).
[παρὰ Πωοῦτος Πα]νε̣χάτου τοῦ Παν̣ε̣χ̣άτου
[μητρὸς . . . . τ]ῆς καὶ Λυκαινίδος τῶν
[ἀπὸ Λύκων πόλ(εως). βού]λ̣(ομαι) πωλ(ῆσαι) τὸ ὑπάρχ(ον) μοι μέρο(ς) γ´
[(ἀρουρῶν) β ἐν τοῖς ἀπὸ νότ(ου) π]εδίοις Λύκων πόλ(εως) ⳨ εἰς τὸ
[. . μο( ) ϛ´ ἀπὸ νότου] κληρονόμων Ἀροννώφριος
[. . . . . . . ἐπὶ τῷ εὐδο]κ̣ε̣[ῖ]ν τὴν ἀδελφὴν Σενποῦν-
[σιν ἕνεκα οὗ ἔχει] μέρους ἡμίσους τῆς κ[α]ρ̣-
[πείας τοῦ μέρου]ς γ´ τῶν (ἀρουρῶν) β ἀκολ(ούθως) τῆι
[. . . . .]χ̣( ) ι̣ε (ἔτους) Ἀ̣ν̣τωνίνου
[Καίσαρος τοῦ κυ]ρ̣[ίου, Φα]ῶ̣φι θ̅. διὸ ἀνα-
[φέρω ὅπως ἐπ]ι̣στείλη̣ς τῶι μνήμ(ονι)
[χρηματίσαι μοι ὡ]ς [κ]α̣θήκει καὶ
[ὀμνύω τὴν] Α̣ὐτοκράτορος Καίσαρος
[Τίτου Αἰλίου] Ἁ̣δ̣ριανοῦ Ἀντωνίνου
[Σεβαστοῦ Εὐσεβοῦς τύχ]η̣ν μ̣ηδενὶ
[ὑποκεῖσθαι. (ἔτους) κδ Αὐτοκ]ρ̣[ά]τ̣ορος Καίσαρ̣ος
[Τίτου Αἰλίου Ἁδ]ρ̣ι̣α̣νοῦ Ἀντωνίνου
[Σεβαστοῦ Εὐσεβοῦς] Φαῶφι ιϛ̅.
[(*m.* 2) Πωοῦς Πανεχάτου ἐπι]δ̣έ̣δ̣ω̣κ̣α̣. (*m.* 3) Σενποῦνσις Πανεχάτ̣(ου)
[μετὰ κυρίου ἐμοῦ τοῦ συγγ(ενοῦς) Ὡρίω]νος Εὐδαίμονος
[εὐδοκῶ ὡς πρόκειται.]

2 βιβ]$^{\lambda}$ ενκ$^{\tau}$; l. ἐγκτ– | Λυκο$^{\pi}$ || **5** Βου]$^{\lambda}$ | π̣ω̣$^{\lambda}$ | υπαρ$^{\chi}$ || **6** πο$^{\lambda}$ || **8** ευδο$^{\kappa}$ || **10** ⳨ | [α]κο$^{\lambda}$ || **11** L || **13** μνη$^{\mu}$

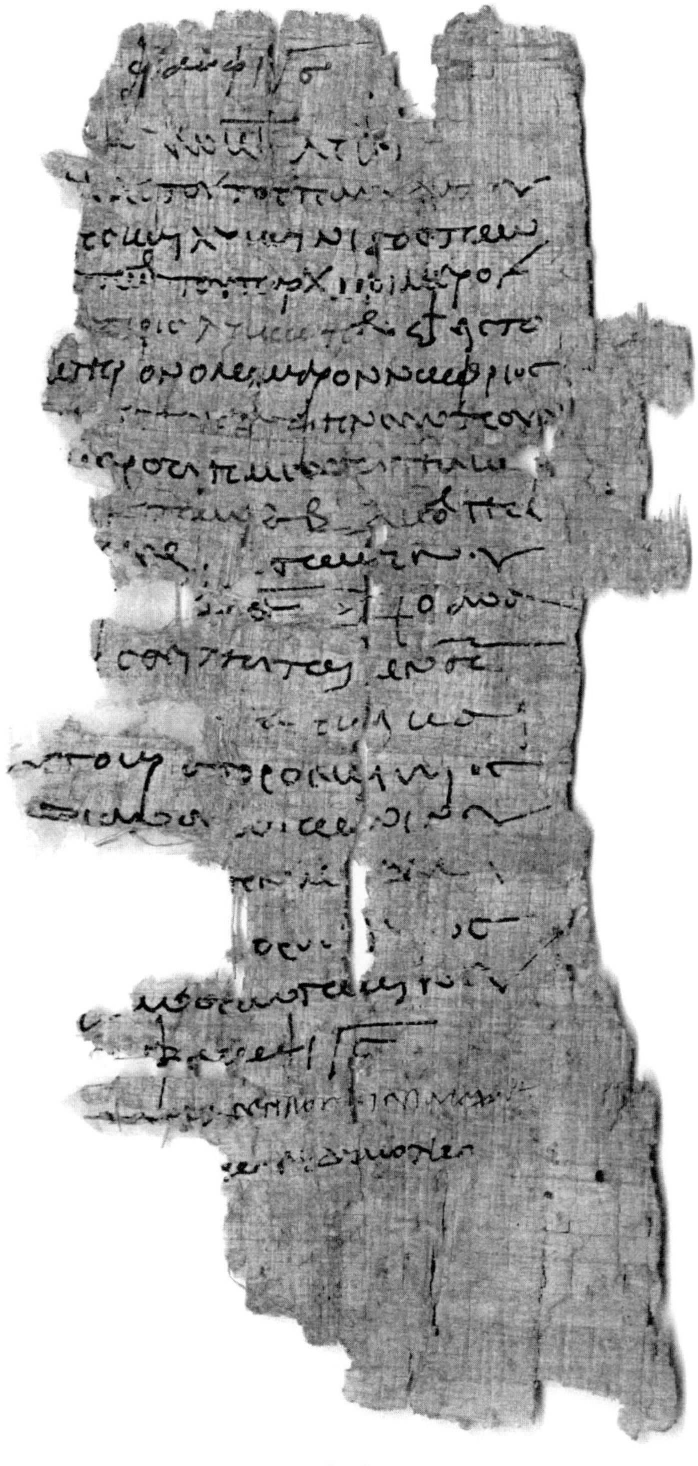

[98]

TRANSLATION

(4th hand) I NN have signed, year 24 Phaophi 16. (1st hand) To NN keeper of the archives of landed property of the Lykopolite. From Poous son of Panechates, grandson of Panechates his mother being NN alias Lykainis, from Lykoplis. I wish to sell the third part of two arouras that belong to me in the southern plains of Lykopolis 3/4 (?) to (?), [1/6 to the south] of the land of the heirs of Haronnophris, with the consent of my sister Senpounsis regarding the half share of the usufruct that she holds in accordance with... the 15th year of Antoninus Caesar, the lord, on the 9th of Phaophi. I therefore give notice in order that you may send instructions to the registrar to issue the document for me, as it should be, and I swear by the fortune of Imperator Caesar Titus Aelius Hadrianus Antoninus Augustus Pius that it is not liable to anyone. The 24th year of Imperator Caesar Titus Aelius Hadrianus Antoninus Augustus Pius, Phaophi the 16th. (2nd hand) I Poous son of Panechates have submitted (this notification). (3rd hand) I Senpounsis daughter of Panechates with my guardian, my relative Horion son of Eudaimon, give my approval as set forth above.

COMMENTARY

4. [μητρός]: I assume that the word was written in full contrary to the supplement in **97**, 4 to allow for the same ca. 7 letters in **97**, 4 to accommodate the mother's name.

6. The sign ʋ at the end of this line does not appear in **97** but is discussed there in the commentary on line 7.

7–8. Ἀροννώφριος | [. . . . . . . : possibly the name of the father of Haronnophris stood at the beginning of line 8. It was apparently omitted in **97**, 7–8.

21–22. The length of these two lines is greater than the average length of the previous lines, therefore one must assume that the subscriptions were written in *ekthesis*.

99. Two Declarations of Sheep and Goats from a *tomos synkollesimos*

P.Fouad inv. 148	w 9.5 × h 14.3 cm	177/178 CE
+ P.Heid. G 1768		
Ptolemais Euergetis		

99 consists of parts of two sheets from a *tomos synkollesimos*. On the upper left are the ends of several lines of writing from the top of one of those sheets. It is pasted onto the left side of another sheet that contains 13 extant lines. **99** provides the missing parts of *P.Heid.* IV 302, which contains parts of the same two sheets from the same *tomos synkollesimos*. **99** contains the right sides of lines 1 and 3–6 of the first sheet of *P.Heid.* 302 and all of what is missing from the top of its second. The following photomontage of the darker image of **99** and the lighter image of *P.Heid.* 302[1] shows how the two pieces fit together:

1. The different brightness of the two images is doubtless mainly due to the different ways that the two papyri were imaged rather than their state of preservation, for the papyri doubtless came from the same dealer before they entered the respective collections, see below, pp. 58–59.

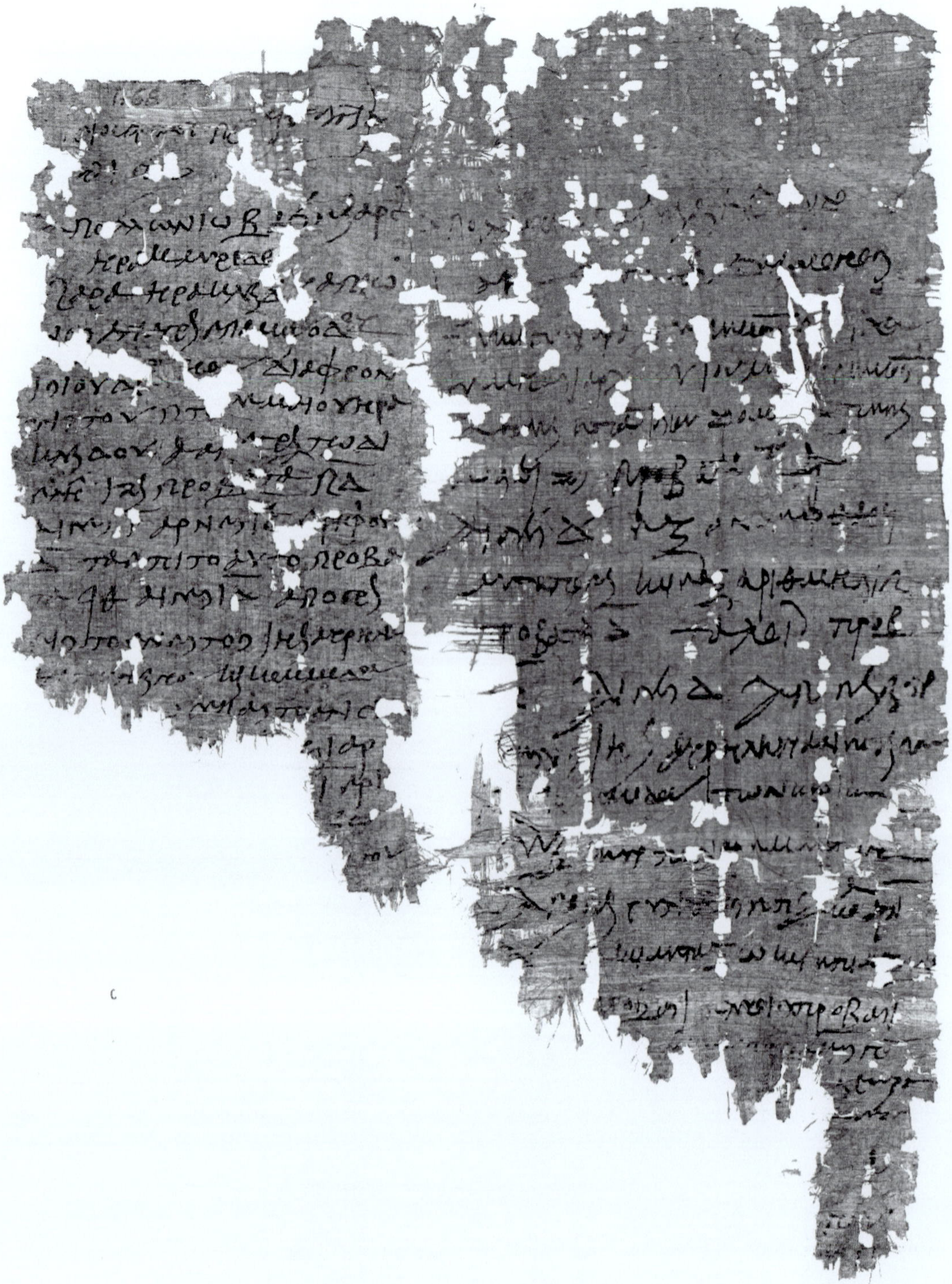

[99 P.Heid. G 1768 + P.Fouad inv. 148]

No explicit information is available about the acquisition of *P.Heid.* IV 302 (inv. G 1768), but since the inventory cards for G 1765 and 1766 indicate "Schubart 1926", it is highly likely that the G 1768 entered the Heidelberg papyrus collection at about this time or shortly afterwards.[2]

2. I am thankful to A. Jördens for this information, she also adds that the cataloging was not carried out regularly, so that no security can be obtained.

The Fouad piece was certainly acquired by the Société by 1939 and probably already by King Fouad from the dealer Nahman in 1930 (see above, introduction, pp. 3–4). It is not certain, but quite likely, that both pieces were purchased from Nahman about 1930.

Both **99** and *P.Heid.* 302 show a *kollesis* with a breadth of over 2 cm. The writing on both sheets runs along the fibers on the recto, but as explained below, the hands are different. On the back of **99** is a docket written across the fibers (see comm.). The back of *P.Heid.* 302 is blank.

Both sheets contain declarations of sheep and goats dated to the 18th year of Marcus Aurelius and Commodus (177–178 CE). The first is by Herakleides son of Apion and is made through his agent (*phrontistes*) Ptolemaios son of Herakleides. The second is by Agathos Daimon alias Sosikrates son of Mysthes. Owing to the fragmentary state of *P.Heid.* IV 302, its editor was uncertain about the purpose of the *tomos synkollesimos*, and this was later discussed by T. Kruse.[3] Thanks to the addition of the Fouad fragment we can be sure that the *tomos* contained original declarations kept by the office of the Royal scribe of the meris of Herakleides of the Arsinoite nome. The possibility that these were copies of successive declarations kept by the declarant himself can now be ruled out.[4] As the two declarations are from the Isieiou Dromou quarter of Ptolemais Euergetis, it is highly probable that the *tomos* was arranged geographically.

The two declarations conform to the third type of declaration from the Arsinoite nome according to the classification of such documents as established by Avogadro and reinforced by Balconi and more recently Langellotti.[5] A single declaration was required, probably in the month of Mecheir. The declaration begins by comparing the size of the flock registered in the previous year, noting changes due to deaths and purchases between then and the current registration.

We already know the declarant of the second declaration, Agathos Daimon alias Sosikrates, ex-*kosmetes* and *gymnasiarchos*, son of Mysthes an ex-*kosmetes*. He is the same person who acknowledges receipt of repayment for a debt to two inhabitants of the village of Soknopaiou Nesos through a bank διαγραφή (*SPP* XXII 172, 166 CE). At that time he had not assumed the gymnasiarchal status yet, being only *kosmetes*. His father seems to have never been in a higher position than *kosmetes*.[6] The two recipients in *SPP* XXII 172 are an Alexandrian named Didymos son of Didymos alias Demetrios and a villager named Pabous son of Satabous.

On the same day, on which *SPP* XXII 172 was issued, the same bank issued a similar receipt, *P.Lond.* II 332, in the name of Agathos Daimon's brother Claudianus alias Serenus to the same Alexandrian, Didymos, together with a Tesenouphis son of Tesenouphis, another Tesenouphis son of Tesenouphis, Panephremmis son of Stotoetis and again a Pabous son

3. *P.Heid.* IV 302 introd.; Kruse 2002, pp. 215–217, esp. n. 479. Note also that the heading of the first sheet of *Heid.* was written by a different hand.

4. That both declarations might have been by one declarant is also suggested by Langellotti (2012, p. 148): "*Non sappiamo se il dichiarante sia lo stesso Herakleides che ha registrato il suo gregge in Ars(H). 177. 1.*" In Langellotti's catalogue (2012, pp. 147–148), the two declarations preserved in *P.Heid.* IV 302 are "Ars(H). 177.1" and "Ars(H). 177.2" respectively.

5. Avogadro 1935, p. 149; Balconi 1984, pp. 47–48; Langellotti 2012, pp. 12–14.

6. Another Agathos Daimon alias Sosikrates is attested in *P.Flor.* I 24 (III CE). He is unlikely to be the same person, but he is perhaps a member of the same family.

of Satabous (most likely the same person in *P.Lond.* II 332). All these names are familiar names in Soknopaiou Nesos, and the persons who bore them were probably also *kamelotrophoi*.

These loans seem to be connected with some economic activity of the Mysthes family. The Alexandrian, Didymos, who was mentioned in both receipts, was perhaps the link between the two Mysthes brothers and the *kamelotrophoi* from Soknopaiou Nesos, or their partner in the business. We actually find him earlier in 163 CE in *BGU* II 607 paying in advance to the *kamelotrophoi* from Soknopaiou Nesos the *phoretra* (transportation fees) which they will later receive from the public treasury, a matter that proves his involvement in financing wheat transportation process in the meris of Herakleides, and also stimulates us to speculate that Mysthes family drew at least part of their wealth from investing in the transportation process.

It is noteworthy that Agathos Daimon declares his flock himself, not through an agent (*phrontistes*). In addition, the absence of a shepherd indicates that he preferred indirect administration of his flock through leases.

Sheet 1

(*m.* 2) 'Ισίου Δρόμου. πρ[ό]β̣α̣τ̣α̣ ρ̣θ̣ αἶγ(ες) ιδ
ἄρ(νες) ι ἔρ(ιφοι) δ̣. *vac.*
(*m.* 1) Ἀπολλωνίῳ βασιλ(ικῷ) γρ(αμματεῖ) Ἀρ(σινοΐτου)
Ἡρακλείδου μερίδο[ς.]
παρὰ Ἡρακλείδο̣υ̣ Ἀπίω-
νος ἀναγρ(αφομένου) ἐπ' ἀμφόδου
'Ισίου Δρόμου διὰ φρον-
τιστοῦ Πτ̣ολεμαίου Ἡρα-
κλείδου. ἃ ἀπ̣ε̣γρ(αψάμην) τῷ δι-
εληλ(υθότι) ιζ (ἔτει) πρόβατα πδ
αἶγες ι̅ ἄρνες ιε̅ ἐρίφους
δ̅, τὰ ἐπὶ τὸ αὐτὸ πρόβα-
τα ρθ αἶγες ιδ̅ ἀπογρ(άφομαι)
εἰς τὸ ἐνεστὸς ιη (ἔτος) Αὐρηλίω̣[ν]
Ἀντωνείνου καὶ Κομμόδου
[τῶν κυρίω]ν̣ Σεβαστῶν σ̣ὺ̣ν̣
[καὶ τοῖς ἐπακο]λ̣[ου]θ[ο]ῦσι ἀρ-
[νάσι ὑποτιτθίοις] ι̅ ἐρί-
[φοις δ, ἃ καὶ μετ]ά̣ξω
[εἰς ἃς ἐὰν αἱρῶμαι] τ̣οῦ
[νομοῦ κώμας . . . . . .] . .
- -

3 βασι^λ || **11** l. αἶγας | l. ἄρνας || **13** l. αἶγας

© Institut für Papyrologie, Universität Heidelberg.

[99 P.Heid G 1768. Photo Elke Fuchs]

Sheet 2

→ Ἀπολλωνίῳ βασιλ(ικῷ) γρα(μματεῖ) Ἀρ(σινοΐτου) Ἡρακλ(είδου) μερίδο(ς).
π̣αρὰ Ἀγα̣θ̣ο̣ῦ Δαίμονος
τοῦ καὶ Σωσικρά[το]υς κεκοσμ(ητευκότος) ἐ[νά]ρχου
γυμνασιάρχ[ου] υἱοῦ Μ[υσ]θ̣ο̣ῦ κεκοσμ(ητευκότος)
ἀναγρ(αφομένου) ἐπ᾽ ἀμ(φόδου) Ἰσίου Δρόμ[ου. ἃ] ἀπεγρ(αψάμην)
τῷ διελ(ηλυθότι) ιζ (ἔτει) πρόβατα ξ̅α̅
αἶγες δ´, ἐξ ὧν δ̣ιεφθάρη
μετ᾽ ἀπογρ(αφὴν) καὶ ἐξαρίθμησιν
πρόβατα δ̅, τὰ λοιπ(ὰ) πρόβ(ατα)
[ν̅]ζ̅ αἶγες δ ἀπογρ(άφομαι) εἰς τὸ
[ἐ]ν̣εστὸς ιη (ἔτος) Αὐρηλίων Ἀντωνείνου
κ̣α̣ὶ Κομμόδου τῶν κυρίων
Σεβ[α]στῶν {τῶν θρ̣εμμάτω̣ν}
{ἀπογρα(φὴν)} σὺν τ̣ο̣ῖς ἐπακολ(ουθοῦσι) ἀρν(άσι)
δ´, ἃ καὶ μετάξω καὶ ἐπιμί̣ξω̣
[ἑτέροις] πρόβασι {ἑτέροις πρόβασι}
[εἰς ἃς ἐὰν αἱρ]ῶ̣μα̣ι̣ τ̣ο̣ῦ ν̣ο̣μ̣(οῦ) κώμας νομ(ὰς)
[ποτίστρας. (*m.* 2) Ἀγαθὸς Δαίμων ὁ κ]αὶ Σ̣ω̣σ̣ι̣κρά–
[της . . . .] ἐ̣[πι]δ̣έ̣δ̣ω̣[κα]
[–ca.?–] . .
[ἔτους ιη Αὐρηλίων Ἀντωνε]ί̣νου
[καὶ Κομμόδου τῶν κυρ]ί̣ω̣ν̣

- -

7, 10 l. αἶγας || **14** ἐπακ$\overset{\lambda}{\text{ο}}$ || **15** l. ἐπιμείξω

Back (on Fouad inv. 148):

↓ (*m.* 3) ἀ̣π̣ο̣γρ(αφὴ) π̣ρ̣ο̣β(άτων)
(κ̣α̣ὶ̣) α̣ἰ̣γ̣ῶ̣ν̣

[99 P.Fouad inv. 148 recto]

[99 P.Fouad inv. 148 verso]

TRANSLATION

SHEET 1

(2nd hand) Of Isieiou Dromou. 99 sheep, 14 goats, 10 lambs, 4 kids. (1st hand) To Apollonios the Royal Scribe of the Arsinoite nome, Herakleides meris from Herakleides son of Apion, registered in Isieiou Dromou quarter, through his representative Ptolemaios son of Herakleides. The 84 sheep, 10 goats, 15 lambs and 4 kids, which I registered in the past 17th year, I register for the present 18th year of Aurelius Antoninus and Aurelius Commodus the lords Augusti in total 99 sheep, 14 goats, with 10 accompanying suckling lambs and 4 kids, which I shall transfer to whatever villages of the nome I choose ...

SHEET 2

To Apollonios the Royal Scribe of the Arsinoite, Herakleides meris, from Agathos Daimon alias Sosikrates, former *kosmetes*, gymnasiarch in office, son of Mysthes, former *kosmetes*, registered in the Isieiou Dromou quarter. Regarding the 61 sheep and 4 goats that I registered in the past 17th year, 4 sheep have died after the registration and counting. The remaining 57 sheep and 4 goats I register for the present 18th year of Aurelius Antoninus and Aurelius Commodus the lords Augusti with the 4 lambs accompanying, which I shall transfer and mingle with other sheep to whatever villages, pastures, and water-holes I choose in the nome. (Hand 2) I Agathos Daimon alias Sosikrates... have submitted... Year 18 of Aurelius Antoninus and Aurelius Commodus the lords...

Verso:
Registration (or Registrations) of sheep and goats.

COMMENTARY

SHEET 1

1. πρόβ̣α̣τ̣α̣ ϙθ̣ αἶγ(ες) ιδ: πρ[(όβατα)][ϙθ αἶγ(ες) ιδ]: *ed. pr.*, most letters supplied by the Fouad piece.
3. γρ(αμματεῖ) Ἀρ(σινοΐτου): supplied by the Fouad piece, [γρ(αμματεῖ)] *ed. pr.*
5. Ἀπίω-: supplied by the Fouad piece.
17. ἐπακο]λ̣[ου]θ̣[ο]ῦσι: instead of ἐπακολουθο]ῦσι (*ed. pr.*)

SHEET 2

4. For the significance of the use of υἱός/θυγάτηρ before the name of the father instead the father's name in the genitive alone for sons and daughters of holders of municipal offices, see Hagedorn 1990, esp. p. 278. Hagedorn points out that when the filiation is given by using υἱός/θυγάτηρ, it was generally because the father was described as holding a respectable social position, usually a municipal or other high office.[7] Cf. *P.Oxy.* LXIV 4438, 10 comm. for exceptions to Hagedorn's rule. Cf. also *P.Oslo* III 144, 9 comm. (with reference to E. Mayser, *Grammatik* II.2, p. 9, n. 3), where the editor gives a wider scope for the use of υἱός/θυγάτηρ asserting that it is "*generally added to avoid accumulation of genitives which*

7. Cf. *P.Lond.* II 376, 1–2 [παρὰ] Διδύμου ἀγορανομ(ήσαντος) υἱο(ῦ) Παπε̣ῶ̣τ̣ο(ς) [. . . .] μητ(ρὸς) αἱρεθέντος. Hagedorn's observations suggest that [. . . .] μητ(ρὸς) in line 2 be changed to [κεκοσ]μητ(ευκότος). See now *BOEP* 8.1, p. 2.

would obscure the family relations, or to confer upon the enumeration a flavor of solemnity, this depending on an old Greek tradition of recording—also when you insist on the titles".

5. Ἰσίου Δρόμ[ου: for Isieiou Dromou Amphodon, a quarter of Ptolemais Euergetis, metropolis of the Arsinoite nome, see Verreth 2013, p. 307 (with further literature). For a list of administrative units of Ptolemais Euergetis in general, see Alston 2002, pp. 381–388. For an outline of the topography of Ptolemais Euergetis, see Casarico 1995, esp. pp. 71–80. For other declarations from the metropolis of the Arsinoite nome, see *P.Heid.* IV 302, 1–2. comm.

8. ἐξ ὧν διεφθάρη | μετ' ἀπογρ(αφὴν) καὶ ἐξαρίθμησιν: similar wording is found in two camel declarations from Soknopaiou Nesos. The one is *SPP* XXII 98 8–10, (170 CE), where μετὰ τὴν [. .] .ἐξαρίθμ(ησιν) διεφθάρη should be changed to μετὰ ἀπογ[ρ(αφὴν) κα]ὶ ἐξαρίθμ(ησιν) διεφθάρη.[8] The other is *BGU* I 266, 11 (217 CE): δ[η]λῶ μετὰ ἀπογρ(αφὴν) καὶ ἐξα[ρίθμησιν. In the declaration of sheep and goats *P.Princ.* II 28, 5–6a (Oxyrhynchos (?), 219 CE), the editor gave ἐξ ὧν διεφθ(άρη) [[πρόβ(ατα)]] \`μετ' ἀ´πογρ(άψασθαι) καὶ ἐξαριθ(μήσασθαι). These two abbreviations, however, should be resolved otherwise: μετ' ἀ|πογρ(αφὴν) καὶ ἐξαρίθ(μησιν).

For a discussion of the process of the enumeration (ἐξαρίθμησις) and the officials involved in it, see Avogadro 1935, pp. 143–146, and especially Langellotti 2012, pp. 14–18. The latter argues that ἐξαρίθμησις no longer means "enumeration" or "counting" but rather "registration", i.e. the cataloging of data relating to the private ownership of sheep and goats by administrative area, a task that was carried out by officials who received the statements. While Langellotti's assumption is plausible, her understanding of the expression μετ' ἀπογραφὴν καὶ ἐξαρίθμησιν is hardly correct. On p. 16 she translates the phrase as "*concordemente al numero registrato ed enumerato.*" Thus understood, however, the words do not account for the reported changes in the size of the flock from one year to the next.

12. καὶ Κομμόδου τῶν κυρίων is mostly on Fouad inv. 148. *P.Heid.* IV 302, 22 has Κ[ο]μ[μόδου τῶν κυρίω]ν.

10–14. εἰς τὸ [ἐ]νεστὸς ιη (ἔτος)... {τῶν θρεμμάτων ἀπογρα(φὴν)}: rather than εἰς <τὴν> το<ῦ> | [ἐ]νεσ<τῶ>τος ιη (ἔτος)... τῶν θρεμμάτων ἀπογρα(φήν). This follows the example of sheet 1, lines 14 ff., and almost all declarations of sheep and goats except *P.Oxy.* XLVII 3338, 9–11 (Arsinoite, but found in Oxyrhynchos, 150 CE): {ἃ καὶ} ἀπογρ(άφομαι) εἰς τὴν τοῦ ἐνεστ[ῶτος] ιγ (ἔτους) Ἀντωνίνου Καίσαρος τοῦ κυ[ρίου] ἀπογραφήν. Cf. the suggested restoration in *P.Heid.* IV 302 ii 22–23 comm.: [ἃ καὶ ἀπογρ(άφομαι) εἰς τὴν τοῦ ἐνεστῶτος. (ἔτους) Αὐρηλίων Ἀντωνείνου καὶ] Κ[ο]μ[μόδου τῶν κυρίω]ν Σεβ[α]-στῶν τῶν [θ]ρ[εμμάτ]ων ἀπογρα(φήν).

14. σὺν τοῖς ἐπακολ(ουθοῦσι) κτλ: on this expression, see *P.Oxy.* LXXI 4822, 6 comm. with bibliography.

8. Image: http://papyri.info/ddbdp/stud.pal;22;98. See now *BOEP* 8.1, p. 3.

15–18. ἃ καὶ μετάξω καὶ ἐπιμί̣ξ̣ω̣ | [ἑτέροις] πρόβασι {ἑτέροις πρόβασι} | [εἰς ἃς ἐὰν αἰρ]ῶ̣μα̣ι̣ τ̣ο̣ῦ ν̣ο̣μ̣(οῦ) κώμας νομ(ὰς) | [ποτίστρα: what is now line 17, *P.Heid.* IV 302 had [–ca.?–] . . . . ν̣ο̣μ̣( ) . . μ̣ .ς νομ( ). Parallel documents contain statements about the owner's rights to pasture animals anywhere in the nome. Cf. sheet 1, 19–21: ἃ καὶ μετ]ά̣ξω | [εἰς ἃς ἐὰν αἰρῶμαι] τ̣οῦ | [νομοῦ κώμας, *P.Mich.* XVIII 782, 6–9 (Arsinoite?, I CE): μετάξω τ̣ὲ̣ (l. δὲ) εἰς ἃς ἐὰν α̣ἰρῶμαι τοῦ νομοῦ κώμαις (l. κώμας) καὶ νομαὶς (νομὰς) καὶ ποτίστραις (l. ποτίστρας) ἐπιμίξω (l. ἐπιμείξω) τ̣ε̣ ἑτέροις πρόβασιν, *BGU* XV 2489, 5–6 (Arsinoite, 134/5 CE): μετάξω ὅπω̣ (l. ὅπου)| ἐὴν (l. ἂν) αἱρῶμαι, and *P.Alex.Giss.* 4 (Euhemeria, 140 CE): [καὶ μετάξω κ]α̣ὶ̣ ἐπιμίξω ἑτέροις [πρόβασι ὧν ποι]μὴν ἐγὼ ὁ Λύκος. [εἰς ἃς ἐὰν αἰρ]ῶ̣μα̣ι̣ τ̣ο̣ῦ ν̣ο̣μ̣(οῦ) κώμας νομ(ὰς) | [ποτίστρας; cf. also *SB* XXII 15780, 9–10 (CE 144/5, Arsinoite): εἰς ἃς ἐὰν α̣ἱρῶμαι [τοῦ νο]μοῦ κώμας νομὰς ποτίστρας and *P.Oxy.* XLVII 3338, 14–15 (Arsinoite, 150 CE): εἰς ἃς ἐὰν αἱρῶμαι τοῦ νο[μοῦ] κώμας νομὰς ποτίστρα[ς; for different formulations typical of individual nomes, see Hagedorn 1976. Cf. *BGU* XVI 2578, 14–16 comm.

18–19. [ποτίστρας (*m.* 2) Ἀγαθὸς Δαίμων ὁ κ]αὶ Σ̣ω̣σ̣ι̣κρά|[της . . . .] ἐ̣[πι]δ̣έ̣δ̣ω̣[κα]: (*m.* 4) [–ca.?–] . . . . ρα| [–ca.?–] . [. .] . . . . *ed. pr.* (lines 28–29): the signature is written in *Verschleifung*. The subscription of a declarant is attested in two other sheep declarations: *P.Oxy.* XLVII 3338 (Ptolemais Euergetis, 150 CE) and *P.Princ.* II 28 (Oxyrhynchos (?), 219 CE). In addition to these two examples, the editor of *P.Stras.* IV 240 (Arsinoite, 147 CE), in his commentary on line 17, suggested that a subscription of the declarant is expected. This understanding was later questioned by Hagedorn (1976, p. 161, n. 8), since no declarant's subscription is attested in declarations from the Arsinoite. Hagedorn's observation, however, ignores the fact that the aforementioned *P.Oxy.* XLVII 3338, found in Oxyrhynchos, actually comes from the Arsinoite. For *P.Stras.* IV 240, see Kruse 2002, p. 219, n. 485.

21. [(ἔτους) ιη Αὐρηλίων Ἀντωνε]ί̣νου: (*m.* 5) [(ἔτους) . Αὐρηλίων Ἀντωνε]ί̣νου *ed. pr.* (line 30): the space could accommodate ἔτους written in full, but the line could have been written in *eisthesis*.

22. The month should be early Mecheir, see Balconi 1984, p. 48 and n. 37.

Verso of sheet 2 (back of P.Fouad inv. 148)

ἀ̣π̣ογρ(αφὴ) π̣ρ̣οβ(άτων) | (κ̣α̣ὶ̣) α̣ἰγ̣ῶ̣ν̣: the docket on the back of sheet 2, identifying its contents, might have been written by the declarant or by one of several officials prior to its having been added to the *tomos* in the office of the *basilikos grammateus*. One might also consider plural ἀ̣π̣ογρ(αφαί), in which case sheet 2 is the last (outer) sheet of the *tomos*. In this case, the docket would have been written in the office of the *basilikos grammateus* and would identify the contents of the entire roll. One should think, however, that such a docket would also specify the geographical area of the registrations (see above, p. 59) and perhaps also the period of time that it covered.

100. Permission to Distrain a Pledge

P.Fouad inv. 252 B — w 10 × h 12 cm — 29.6.211 CE
Lykopolite (?)

The upper left corner of the document is preserved. The writing runs along the fibers on the recto. The back is blank. That the papyrus was written in the Lykopolite nome is likely by reason of its inventory number 252 B, for 252 A (**97** in this volume) is from the Lykopolite nome as are the nearby inv. numbers.[1]

A certain Neilos son of Agathos Daimon is trying to reclaim a debt from an unknown person. Since the debtor had failed to repay the debt, Neilos had to go through the long route of seizing the collateral.[2]

In the present document, Neilos forwards a copy of a document that he had received from the office of the chief judge in Alexandria (ἀρχιδικαστής).[3] Since the addressee in the present document appears to be omitted, we are probably dealing with a copy that was made for Neilos' personal records (see comm. on l. 1).

Neilos had initiated the process by petitioning the prefect, requesting distraint of the pledge. Then the judicial authorities, the *chrematistai*, after examining the case, wrote to the *strategos* and the *praktor xenikon*, authorizing them to proceed to seize the pledge. The document that Neilos is forwarding is this authorization of distraint of the pledge (ἐνεχυρασίας χρηματισμός). It is addressed by the chief judge to the *praktor xenikon*.[4] Similar authorizations addressed to the *praktor xenikon* are *P.Thomas* 13 (185 CE), *PSI* XIII 1328 (201 CE) and *P.Heid.* IV 325 (215 CE). These documents, all of them from Oxyrhynchos (see comm. on lines 1–2), are what is referred to as the "parallels" in the commentary below.

100, like its parallels, presents the procedure in reverse chronological order. The structure of the document is as follows:

1. On invs. 228–257, see the introduction, pp. 3–4.
2. The procedure is summarized by Taubenschlag (1944 (ed. 1955), pp. 531–537); see also Schwarz 1937; Kupiszewski 1956; Rupprecht 1997; Rupprecht 2014, pp. 259–265.
3. Usually through the καταλογεῖον (the record office of legal judgements), or, as in our case, the διαλογή (a sub-department of the καταλογεῖον). On the functions of the καταλογεῖον and the διαλογή see Koschaker 1907, *esp.* pp. 264–270; Wilcken 1908, pp. 372–373; Holton 1968; Wolff 1978, pp. 28, 249–250, n. 12.
4. Various interpretations have been offered for the origin and meaning of the second term in the title πράκτωρ ξενικῶν. Scholars have suggested that it refers to debts between residents of different nomes; between people not liable to the law of the city (i.e. Alexandria); to non-sacral debts as opposed to debts owed to temples; or, in the Roman period, as equivalent to *inter peregrinos*. See Płodzień 1951; Préaux 1955; Rabinowitz 1957–1958, pp. 180–181; *P.Thomas*, p. 145, n. 3; cf. also *P.Lips.* I 120 introd. The glossary in Keenan, Manning, Yiftach-Firanko 2014, p. 559 s.v., provides the following definition: "*A type of tax-collector, also concerned with the execution of loans secured by mortgage and the auction sale of such property in cases of default.*"

Lines 1–3: A notification by the plaintiff, Neilos, almost certainly to the *praktor xenikon*, that he is forwarding a copy of an authorization of distraint which he had drawn up from the office of the chief judge (ἀρχιδικαστής), cf. comm. on line 1.

Lines 3–6: A communication by the chief judge to the *praktor xenikon*, instructing him to execute the decision made by the *chrematistai* in court proceedings that dealt with Neilos' petition. In doing so the chief judge includes a copy of the court minutes.

Lines 6–16: A copy of the aforementioned minutes of the *chrematistai*, mentioning the reading of Neilos' petition and pertinent documents, in the presence of his legal representative, and their decision to inform the *strategos* and the *praktor xenikon* (both presumably of the Lykopolite nome) that the creditor should provide a document containing a sworn confirmation of the accuracy of the petition before a copy of the documents (i.e. the sworn confirmation and the authorization of distraint) are personally served on the debtor. And they add that if the debtor does not file a defense within ten days, one should proceed to the seizure of the pledged asset.

Line 17: Shortly after the commencement of the quotation of the earliest step of the procedure, i.e. the petition to the prefect, in which the prerequisite for the application to execute the pledge was set forth, the text breaks off.

→ Παρὰ Νείλου Ἀγαθοῦ Δ[αίμονος ....]
παρακομισθέντα ἀπὸ διαλογῆς ἐνεχυρασί[ας χρηματισμὸν περὶ τῶν ....με-]
νων μοι οὕτως ἔχοντα· *vac.* ξενικῶν π[ράκτορι Λυκοπολ(ίτου). τῆς τετελ(ειωμένης) ἐνεχυρασίας ἐστιν]
ἀντίγρ(αφον). Ἐπιτελεσθήτω καθότι συνκέκριτ[αι. ἔτους ιθ Μάρκου Αὐρηλίου Ἀντωνίνου καὶ Πουβλίου]
Σεπτιμίου Γέτα Εὐσεβῶν Σεβαστῶν Ἐ[π]εὶφ ε̅ [signature...]
ἔτους ẹ[ν]νεακαιδẹḳάτọυ Ạ[ὐτοκρατόρων Καισάρων Μάρκου Αὐρηλίου Ἀντωνίνου καὶ Πουβλίου]
Σεπτιμ[ίου Γ]έτα Βρεταạ[ννικῶν μεγίστων Εὐσεβῶν Σεβαστῶν, Ἐπεὶφ .. ἀναγνωσθείσης ἐντεύξεως Νείλου]
Ἀγαθοῦ Δ[αί]μονος, τῆς δὲ δị' ạ[ὐτ]ῆṣ [ση]μạịṿ[ομένης ....χρημα-]
[τι]σμοῦ ὑπογεγραμμένου ἐπενηνεγμένου, [καὶ τοῦ λεγομένου διαπεστάλθαι ΝΝ]
[ὑπο]γεγραφότος διαπεστάλθαι πρὸς τὴν τοῦ χ̣[ρηματισμοῦ τελείωσιν, συνεκρίναμεν γραφῆ-]
[ναι] καὶ πεμφθῆναι τῆς ἐντεύξεως ἀντίγ[ρ(αφον) τοῖς τοῦ Λυκοπολίτου στρατηγῷ καὶ ξενικῶν]
[πρά]κ̣τορι̣, ἵν', ἐὰν παρῶ<ν> ἐπ' α[ὐτο]ὺς ὁ Νεῖḷọṣ ẹὐ̣[δοκῇ τούτοις καὶ προῆται τὴν καθήκουσαν χειρογ(ραφίαν)]
[πε]ρ̣ὶ̣ [το]ῦ̣ [ἀλη]θῆ [ε]ἶ̣ναι τὰ διὰ τῆς ἐντεύξεω̣[ς δεδηλωμένα καὶ μηδὲν ὑπεναντίον ᾠκονομῆσθαι]
[μη]δ̣ὲ ἔχειν τι εἰς τὰ πρασσόμενα, ἀπ[ερίλυτον δὲ εἶναι τὴν ὀφειλήν, τὸ τηνικαῦτα μεταδοθέντος τῶν]

[γρα]μ̣μ̣άτων τούτων ἀντιγρ[άφου] τῷ δ̣ι̣ὰ̣ [τῆς ἐντεύξεως διασαφουμένῳ ἐνωπίῳ, ἵν᾽ εἰδῇ, καὶ ἂν μηδὲν]
[ἀντ]είπῃ ἐν ἡμέραις δέκα, μετὰ ταύτας συγ̣[τελῶσι τὰ τῆς πράξεως ὃν τρόπον καθήκει τοῖς προστεταγμέ-]
[νοις] ἀ̣κ̣ο̣λ̣ο̣ύ̣θως. vac. Σουβατι̣α̣ν̣ῷ [Ἀκύλα̣ …]
- -

4 αντιγρ/

[100]

TRANSLATION

... from Neilos son of Agathos Daimon... The authorization of distraint concerning... which had been conveyed to me from the bureau is as follows: To the *praktor xenikon* of the Lykopolite(?) nome. A copy of the authorization of distraint which had been executed follows. Let it be done as it had been judged. The 19th year of Marcus Aurelius Antoninus and Publius Septimius Geta Pii Augusti, Epeiph the 5th... The nineteenth year of Emperors Caesars Marcus Aurelius Antoninus and Publius Septimius Geta Britannici maximi Pii Augusti, Epeiph... A petition of Neilos son of Agathos Daimon having been read and the communication cited below about the..., which is indicated in the petition, having been produced, and NN, who was stated to be his representative, having added the subscription that he has been appointed as a representative for the execution of the bill of restraint..., we have decided that a copy of the petition be made and sent to the *strategos* of the Lykopolite(?) nome and to the *praktor xenikon* with the following intent: if in their presence Neilos agrees to this and having declared on oath that the evidence presented in the petition is true and that no impeding arrangement at all has been made and that no further transaction affecting the case is in progress, but that the debt is uncancelled, in that case they deliver a copy of these documents to the debtor, who is specified in the petition, so that he may be informed, and, if he does not make answer within ten days, that they after that time complete the process of execution in whatever manner is proper, according to the instructions. To Subatianus Aquila...

COMMENTARY

1. There should be a preceding line indicating the addressee. Hence, what appears to be a margin above the first line of the text might be blank space following mention of the addressee. If the addressee was omitted, the document was probably a copy made for and kept by the applicant. For a similar explanation of census returns without addressees, cf. BAGNALL 1994, p. 120; DUTTENHÖFER 1997, p. 57. Parallel communications from the Oxyrhynchite are addressed to the overseer(s) of the ξενικὴ πρακτορία[5] and to a contractor (δημοσιώνης).[6] At the end of line 1 will have stood a verb—e.g. ὑπέταξα—governing the accusative masculine singular or neuter plural in line 2.

2–3. παρακομισθέντα ἀπὸ διαλογῆς ἐναςυρασί[ας χρηματισμὸν (or γράμματα) περὶ τῶν - - - οὕτως ἔχοντα: there is no precise parallel. We seem to be dealing with a local variant of similar phrases found in other documents with other provenances. Communications to the πράκτωρ ξενικῶν from Oxyrhynchos use the active form ἐπορίσα to express very much the same, i.e. οὗ ἐπόρισα ἐκ τοῦ καταλογείου ἐνεχυρασίας χρηματισμοῦ ἐστιν ἀντίγραφον as

5. Cf., e.g., *P.Thomas* 13, 1–2 (Oxyrhynchos, 183 CE): Σαραπίωνι καὶ Ἁρποκρατίωνι [ἐπιτηρηταῖς τῆς ἐν Ὀξυρυγχ(ίτῃ) ξε]νικῆς πρακτορείας and *PSI* XIII 1328, 1 (Oxyrhynchos, 201 CE): Σαραπίωνι ἐπιτηρητῇ ξενικῆς πρακτορείας Ὀξυρυγχ(είτου).

6. Cf. *P.Heid.* IV 325, 1–2 (Oxyrhynchite, 215 CE): δημοσιών[η ξ]ενικῆς | [πρακτορείας Ὀξυρυγχείτου].

in *P.Thomas* 13, 3–4 (183 CE), *PSI* XIII 1328, 4 (201 CE) and *P.Heid.* IV 325, 4–5 (215 CE). Communications to the *strategos* from the Arsinoite and the Hermopolite use the active form παρεκόμισα; so *BGU* IV 1038, 9 (Arsinoite, 144 CE), *BGU* XV 2472, 5 (Arsinoite, 159/60 CE) and *P.Flor.* I 56, 2–3 (Hermopolite, 233/34 CE). For the passive, cf. *BGU* VII 1573, 1 (Philadelphia, 141 CE): τοῦ παρακομισθέντος ἀπὸ διαλογῆς χρηματισμοῦ ἐ̣μ̣β[αδείας (also line 14).

For the possibility of παρακομισθέντα - - - ἐνεχυρασί[ας γράμματα, cf. *P.Oxy.* XLIX 3468, 14–15 (Oxyrhynchos, I CE): ἐτόλμ̣ησεν ἐπιτελέσαι κατ' αὐτοῦ γρ̣ά̣μματα ἐνεχυρασίας.

3. The restoration of Λυκοπολ(ίτου) / Λυκοπολίτου in the present line and in 11 is likely, see above, p. 68 with n. 1.

4. ἐπιτελεσθήτω καθότι συνκέκριται: cf. *PSI* XIII 1310, 4 (Arsinoite, 146–145 or 135–134 BCE): ἐπιτελε[σθήτω οὖν καθὼς σ]υγκέκριτα[ι. c ?], and 1328, 6 (Oxyrhynchos, 201 CE) τελεσθήτω καθότι συνκέκριται.

8–9. τῆς δὲ δι̣' α̣[ὐτ]ῆ̣ς̣ [ση]μ̣α̣ι̣ν̣[ομένης - - - χρημα]|[τι]σμοῦ ὑπογεγραμμένου ἐπενηνεγμένου: in the phrase δι̣' α̣[ὐτ]ῆ̣ς, the prepositon refers to the aforementioned ἔντευξις. In it was indicated ([ση]μ̣α̣ι̣ν̣[ομένης) another document. Parallels suggest that it was one of the following:

(a) a διαγραφή (i.e. bank receipt): cf. *P.Aberd.* 19, 7 (Arsinoite, II–III CE): [τῆς δὲ] δι' α[ὐτο]ῦ̣[7] σημαινομένης δι[α]γραφ[ῆς ἐπενηνεγμένης.

(b) a συγγραφή (i.e. the contract itself): cf. *P.Fam.Tebt.* 29, 8–10 (Tebtynis, 133 CE): τῆς [δὲ δι' αὐτ]ῆ̣ς σημαινομένης συνγραφῆς ὑπογεγραμμένης ἐκ [τῆς τοῦ Ναν]αίου̣ βιβλιοθήκης ἐπενηνεγμένης.

(c) a δημοσίωσις (i.e. publication): cf. *P.Heid.* IV 325, 12–13 (Oxyrhynchite, 215 CE): τῶν δὲ δι' αὐτῆς σημαινο]μένων ὑπομνημάτ[ων] π̣ε̣ρ̣ὶ̣ δη[μ]οσ[ιώσεως χειρογράφου ὡς καθήκει ὑπο]γεγ[ρ]α̣μ̣μένων ἐ̣π̣ε̣ν̣η̣νεγμέ̣[νων].

(d) a combination of several documents; cf. *P.Thomas* 13, 11–13 (Oxyrhynchos, 183 CE): τῶν δὲ δι' αὐτῆς σημαινομέ̣νων διαγραφῆ̣[ς] καὶ δημ[ο]σ̣ι̣ώ̣σ̣εω̣ς καὶ ἀντιφωνήσεως ὑπογεγραμμένων ἐκ τῆς δ[η(μοσίας) βι]βλιοθή[κης] ἐ̣π̣ε̣ν̣η̣ν̣[εγμένων]; *PSI* XIII 1328, 13–16 (Oxyrhynchos, 201 CE): τοῦ δὲ δι' αὐτῆς σημαινομένου ὑπομνήματος περὶ δημοσιώσεως χειρογράφου ὑπογεγραμμένου καὶ ἐκδοσίμου ὑφ' ὅ εἰσιν καὶ αἱ μεταδόσεως ὑπογραφαὶ ἐπενηνεγμένων.

Since the copy of the original petition to the prefect is not preserved, it is hard to tell which of the aforementioned documents is meant. H. Cuvigny suggests *per litteras* that if there was a document of δημοσίωσις, then the contract which the creditor showed to the χρηματισταί can only be a χειρόγραφον, not a notarial συγγραφή or a bank διαγραφή. She suggests that [ση]μ̣α̣ι̣ν̣[ομένης probably refers to a ἰδιόγραφος συγγραφή, i.e. a non-notarial contract typical of Oxyrhynchos. Therefore, Cuvigny would thus supplement σημαινομένης συγγραφῆς καὶ δημοσιώσεως χρηματισμοῦ.

7. Probably to be changed to α[ὐτῆ]ς in reference to the ἔντευξις mentioned in the previous line. Also in *P.Laur.* IV 160, 6–7 (Provenance unknown, 138–161 CE) τῆς δὲ [δι' αὐτοῦ δεδηλωμένης the pronoun should be changed to αὐτῆς, likewise in reference to an aforementioned ἔντευξις.

12. τὴν καθήκουσαν χειρογ(ραφίαν): restored with all the parallels, cf., e.g., *P.Flor.* I 56, 17–18 (Hermopolite, 88 CE): τὴν ἁρμόζουσαν χειρογραφίαν. The abbreviation χειρογ(ραφίαν) is given *exempli gratia* for reasons of space. The χειρογραφία is a written account of the debt under oath; cf., e.g., *BGU* IV 1038, 5–6 (Arsinoite, 144 CE), where the oath repeats the wordings of the ἐνεχυρασία: κα̣ὶ̣ ὀμ̣ν̣ύ̣ω̣ [τὴν Ἀντωνί]νου Καίσαρος τοῦ κυ[ρίου τύχην – *ca.* 40 –]σθαι μή[τε ἔ]χειν τι εἰς τὰ πρασσόμενα, ἀπερίλυτον δὲ εἶ[ναι τὴν] ὀφειλήν.

14. ἀπ[ερίλυτον δὲ εἶναι τὴν ὀφειλήν: this phrase is restored with all the parallels (except in *PSI* XIII 1328l, 23, where ταῦτα was used instead of τὴν ὀφειλήν).

16–17. μετὰ ταύτας συ̣ν̣[τελῶσι τὰ τῆς πράξεως ὃν τρόπον καθήκει τοῖς προστεταγμέ]|[νοις] ἀ̣κ̣ο̣λ̣ο̣ύ̣θως: this is restored with all the parallels. Since space is a bit tight, one or two words were probably abbreviated.

Bibliography

ALONSO 2010
Alonso, J.L., "The Bibliotheke Enkteseon and the Alienation of Real Securities in Roman Egypt", *JJP* 40, 2010, pp. 11–54.

ALSTON 2002
Alston, R., *The City in Roman and Byzantine Egypt*, London, New York, 2002.

RI. ALSTON, RO. ALSTON 1997
Alston, R., Alston, R.D., "Urbanism and the Urban Community in Roman Egypt", *JEA* 83, 1997, pp. 199–216.

AVOGADRO 1935
Avogadro, S., "Le ἀπογραφαί di proprieta nell'Egitto Greco-romano", *Aegyptus* 15, 1935, pp. 131–206.

BAGNALL 1994
Bagnall, R.S., "Census Declarations from the British Library", *CdE* 69, 1994, pp. 109–126.

BAGNALL 1997
Bagnall, R.S., "A Mandate from the Great Oasis", *ZPE* 116, 1997, pp. 149–151.

BAGNALL 1998
Bagnall, R.S., "Cults and Names of Ptolemais in Upper Egypt", in W. Clarysse et al. (eds.), *Egyptian Religion: The Last Thousand Years. Studies Dedicated to the Memory of Jan Quaegebeur*, OLA 85, Leuven, 1998, vol. II, pp. 1093–1101.

BAGNALL, FRIER 1994 (ed. 2006)
Bagnall, R.S., Frier, B.W., *The Demography of Roman Egypt* (1994), Cambridge Studies in Population, Economy and Society in Past Time 23, Cambridge, 2006.

BALCONI 1984
Balconi, C., "ΑΠΟΓΡΑΦΑΙ ΠΡΟΒΑΤΩΝ ΚΑΙ ΑΙΓΩΝ dell'età di Tiberio e Caligola", *Aegyptus* 64, 1984, pp. 35–60.

BERGAMASCO 1995
Bergamasco, M., "Le διδασκαλικαί nella ricerca attuale", *Aegyptus* 75, 1995, pp. 95–167.

BERGAMASCO 2004
Bergamasco, M., "Tre note a tre διδασκαλικαί", *SEP* 1, 2004, pp. 31–41.

BOGAERT 1995
Bogaert, R., "Liste géographique des banques et des banquiers de l'Égypte romaine, 30a–284", *ZPE* 109, 1995, pp. 133–173.

BOGAERT 1997
Bogaert, R., "La Banque en Égypte Byzantine", *ZPE* 116, 1997, pp. 85–140.

BOGAERT 2000
Bogaert, R., "Les opérations des banques de l'Égypte romaine", *AncSoc* 30, 2000, pp. 135–209.

BOGAERT 2001
Bogaert, R., "Les documents bancaires de l'Égypte gréco-romaine et byzantine", *AncSoc* 31, 2001, pp. 173–288.

BORRELLI 2016
Borrelli, B., "Riedizione di P.Worp 22: registro di contratti", *Aegyptus* 96, 2016, pp. 17–25.

BRIGUGLIO 2007
Briguglio, F., *Studi sul procurator* I: *L'acquisto del possesso e della proprietà*, Milan, 2007.

BROUX 2014
Broux, Y., *Double Names in Roman Egypt: A Prosopography*, TOP 8, Leuven, 2014.

Broux 2015

Broux, Y., *Double Names and Elite Strategy in Roman Egypt*, StudHell 54, Leuven, 2015.

Bryen 2008

Bryen, A.Z., "Violence, Law and Society in Roman and Late Antique Egypt", PhD Thesis, University of Chicago, 2008.

Bureth 1964

Bureth, P., *Les titulatures impériales dans les papyrus, les ostraca et les inscriptions d'Égypte (30 a.C.–284 p.C.)*, Bruxelles, 1964.

Buzi, Giorgi 2020

Buzi, P., Giorgi, E, *The Urban Landscape of Bakchias: A Town of the Fayyūm from the PtolemaicRoman Period to Late Antiquity*, ARA 66, Oxford, 2020.

Caldara 1924

Caldara, A., *I connotati personali nei documenti dell'età greca e romana*, Milan, 1924.

Casarico 1995

Casarico, L., "La metropoli dell'Arsinoite in epoca romana", *Aevum* 69, 1995, pp. 69–94.

Daris 2000

Daris, S., "I Quartieri di Ossirinco : materiali e note", *ZPE* 132, 2000, pp. 211–221.

Dieter 1964

Dieter, S., *Studien zur Praxis der Stipulationsklausel*, MBPF 48, Munich, 1964.

Döllstädt 1934

Döllstädt, W., "Griechische Papyrusprivatbriefe in gebildeter Sprache aus den ersten vier Jahrhunderten nach Christus", PhD Thesis, University of Jena, Borna/Leipzig, 1934.

Duncan-Jones 1977

Duncan-Jones, R.P., "Age-Rounding, Illiteracy and Social Differentiation in the Roman Empire", *Chiron* 7, 1977, pp. 333–353.

Duttenhöfer 1997

Duttenhöfer, R., "Five Census Returns in the Beinecke Library", *BASP* 34, 1997, pp. 53–78.

Elmaghrabi 2020

Elmaghrabi, M.G., "The Dossier of the Descendants of Zeuxis", in C.E. Römer (ed.), *News from Texts and Archaeology. Acts of the 7th International Fayoum Symposium*, Wiesbaden, 2020, pp. 19–25.

Falivene 1998

Falivene, M., *The Herakleopolite Nome: A Catalogue of the Toponyms, with Introduction and Commentary*, ASP 37, Atlanta, 1998.

Flory 1984

Flory, M.B., "*Sic Exempla Parantur*: Livia's Shrine to Concordia and the Porticus Liviae", *Historia* 33, 1984, pp. 309–330.

Forselv 1998

Forselv, I.L., "Registration of an Apprentice: P. Osl. inv. no. 1470", *SymbOsl* 73, 1998, pp. 116–124.

Fournet 2000

Fournet, J.-L., "Le système des intermédiaires dans les reçus fiscaux byzantins et ses implications chronologiques sur le dossier de Dioscore d'Aphrodité", *APF* 46, 2000, pp. 233–247.

Gascou 1978

Gascou, J., "P.Fouad 87 : les monastères pachômiens et l'État byzantin", *BIFAO* 76, 1978, pp. 157–184.

Gascou 1981

Gascou, J., "Documents grecs relatifs au monastère d'Abba Apollôs de Titkôis", *Anagennesis* l, 1981, pp. 219–230.

Gignac 1981

Gignac, F.T., *A Grammar of the Greek Papyri of the Roman and Byzantine Periods*, 2 vols., Milan, 1981.

Grether 1946

Grether, G., "Livia and the Roman Imperial Cult", *AJP* 67, 1946, pp. 222–252.

Häge 1970

Häge, G., "Die ΜΗ ΕΛΑΤΤΟΥΜΕΝΟΥ–Klausel in den griechischen Papyri Aegyptens", in D.H. Samuel (ed.), *Proceedings of the Twelfth International Congress of Papyrology, Ann Arbor, 13–17 August 1968*, ASP 7, Toronto, 1970, pp. 195–205.

Hagedorn 1976

Hagedorn, D., "Zum Formular der Kleinviehdeklarationen", *ZPE* 21, 1976, pp. 159–165.

Hagedorn 1990

Hagedorn, D., "Zur Verwendung von υἱός und θυγάτηρ vor dem Vatersnamen in Urkunden römischer Zeit", *ZPE* 80, 1990, pp. 277–282.

Hagedorn 2004

Hagedorn, D., "Bemerkungen zu Urkunden", *ZPE* 149, 2004, pp. 159–161.

Hagen, Ryholt 2016

Hagen, F., Ryholt, K., *The Antiquities Trade in Egypt 1880-1930: The H.O. Lange Papers*, Copenhagen, 2016.

Hamza 1984

Hamza, G., "Einige Bemerkungen zur Systasis in den Papyri", in V. Giuffrè (ed.), *Sodalitas: Scritti in onore di Antonio Guarino*, vol. 6, Naples, 1984, pp. 2653–2666.

Harmon 1934

Harmon, A.M., "Egyptian Property Returns", *YCS* 4, 1934, pp. 133–234.

Herrmann 1957–1958

Herrmann, J., "Vertragsinhalt und Rechtsnatur der ΔΙΔΑΣΚΑΛΙΚΑΙ", *JJP* 11–12, 1957–1958, pp. 119–139.

Herrmann 1974

Herrmann, J., "Interpretation von Vollmachtsurkunden", in E. Kiessling, H.-A. Rupprecht (eds.), *Akten des XIII. Internationalen Papyrologenkongresses, Marburg/Lahn, 2–6 August 1971*, MBPF 66, Munich, 1974, pp. 159–167.

Holton 1968

Holton, P.R., "Grapheion, Catalogue, and Library in Roman Egypt", *SymbOsl* 43, 1968, pp. 68–83.

Hübsch 1968

Hübsch, G., *Die Personalangaben als Identifizierungsvermerke im Recht der gräko–ägyptischen Papyri*, Berliner Juristische Abhandlungen 20, Berlin, 1968.

Jördens/Yiftach-Firanko 2010

A. Jördens, "Nochmals zur *Bibliotheke Enkteseon*" and U. Yiftach-Firanko, "Comments on Andrea Jördens, 'Nochmals zur *Bibliotheke Enkteseon*'" in: G. Thür (ed.), *Symposion 2009. Vorträge zur griechischen und hellenistischen Rechtsgeschichte (Seggau, 23.–30. August 2009)*, AGR 21, Vienna 2010, pp. 277–290, 291–299.

Keenan, Manning, Yiftach-Firanko 2014

Keenan, J., Manning, J., Yiftach-Firanko, U. (eds.), *Law and Legal Practice in Egypt from Alexander to the Arab Conquest: A Selection of Papyrological Sources in Translation, with Introductions and Commentary*, Cambridge, 2014.

Kelly 2011

Kelly, B., *Petitions, Litigation, and Social Control in Roman Egypt*, Oxford, 2011.

Koschaker 1907

Koschaker, P., "Der Archidikastes. Beiträge zur Geschichte des Urkunden- und Archivwesens im römischen Ägypten", *ZSSR* 28, 1907, pp. 254–305.

Krüger 1990

Krüger, J., *Oxyrhynchos in der Kaiserzeit: Studien zur Topographie und Literaturrezeption*, Europäische Hochschulschriften, Reihe III, Geschichte und ihre Hilfswissenschaften 441, Frankfurt, 1990.

Kruit 1994

Kruit, N., "Three Byzantine Sales for Future Delivery", *Tyche* 9, 1994, pp. 67–88.

Kruse 2002

Kruse, T., *Der Konigliche Schreiber und die Gauverwaltung: Untersuchungen zur Verwaltungsgeschichte Ägyptens in der Zeit von Augustus bis Philippus Arabs (30 v.Chr.-245 n.Chr.)*, Munich, 2002.

Kupiszewski 1956

Kupiszewski, H., "Les formulaires dans la procédure d'exécution", *Symbolae Raphaeli Taubenschlag dedicatae* (= *Eos* 48, [1956]), pp. 89–103.

Langellotti 2012

Langellotti, M., *L'allevamento di pecore e capre nell'Egitto romano. Aspetti economici e sociali*, Pragmateiai 21, Bari, 2012.

Lenger 1950–1951

Lenger, M.-T., "Un Papyrus d'Eschine : Contre Timarque, §§ 53–54", in *Mélanges Joseph Hombert*, *Phoibos* 5, 1950–1951, pp. 87–93.

Lenger 1951

Lenger, M.-T., "Fragment d'ὑπόμνημα du IIe siècle avant J.-C.", in *Raccolta di scritti in onore di Girolamo Vitelli* 1, *Aegyptus* 31, 1951, pp. 246–253.

Lewis 1944 (ed. 1995)

Lewis, N., "The Meaning of σὺν ἡμιολίᾳ and Kindred Expressions in Loan Contracts", *TAPA* 76, 1944, pp. 126–139 (= Lewis, N., *On Government and Law in Roman Egypt*, Atlanta, 1995, pp. 17–30).

Lobel, Page 1952

Lobel, E., Page, D.L., "A New Fragment of Aeolic Verse", *CQ* 46 , 1952, pp. 1–3.

Lolos 2005
Lolos, Y., "Greek Roads: A Commentary on the Ancient Terms", *Glotta* 79, 2003 [2005], pp. 137–174.

Maresch 2002
Maresch, K., "Die Bibliotheke Enkteseon im römischen Ägypten", *APF* 48, 2002, pp. 233–246.

Markiewicz 2006
Markiewicz, T., "Heqanakhte and the Origins of *Hemiolion*", *JJP* 36, 2006, pp. 125–136.

Mascellari 2021
Mascellari, R., *La lingua delle petizioni nell'Egitto romano: Evoluzione di lessico, formule e procedure dal 30 a.C. al 300 d.C*, Edizioni dell'Istituto Papirologico «G. Vitelli» 11,Florence, 2021.

Mascellari 2018
Mascellari, R., "Il saluto finale delle petizioni nei papiri di epoca romana: da εὐτύχει a διευτύχει", *APF* 64, 2018, pp. 294–305.

van Minnen 1993
Minnen, P. van, "Notes on Texts from Graeco-Roman Egypt", *ZPE* 96, 1993, pp. 117-122.

Montevecchi 1998
Montevecchi, O., "La provenienza di P.Oxy. 984", *Aegyptus* 78, 1998, pp. 49–76.

Montevecchi 2000
Montevecchi, O., "Ancora su Lycopolis", *Aegyptus* 80, 2000, pp. 145–146.

Ogden 1990
Ogden, J.M., "Gold Jewellery in Ptolemaic, Roman and Byzantine Egypt", PhD Thesis, Durham University, 1990.

Packman 1994
Packman, Z.M., "Still Further Notes on Papyrus Documents with the Imperial Oath", *ZPE* 100, 1994, pp. 207–210.

Papathomopoulos 1961
Papathomopoulos, M., "Un Fragment sur Papyrus de Démosthène (Contre Dionysodoros 47–50)", RechPap 1, Paris, 1961, pp. 37–39.

Papathomopoulos 1964
Papathomopoulos, M., "Un Argument sur Papyrus de la Médée d'Euripide", RechPap 3, Paris, 1964, pp. 37–47.

Passoni Dell'Acqua 1982
Passoni Dell'Acqua, A., "Mandato (ΑΠΟΣΥΣΤΑΤΙΚΟΝ), P.Med. inv. 50", *Anagennesis* 2, 1982, pp. 131–137.

Perdicoyianni-Paleologou 1999
Perdicoyianni-Paleologou, H., "Les contrats d'apprentissage en provenance d'Oxyrhynchos", *AntClass* 68, 1999, pp. 149–169.

Perdrizet 1931
Perdrizet, P., "Le jeu alexandrin de l'icosaèdre", *BIFAO* 30, 1931, pp. 1–16.

Płodzień 1951
Płodzień, S., "The Origin and Competence of the πράκτωρ ξενικών", *JJP* 5, 1951, pp. 217–227.

Préaux 1955
Préaux, C., "Sur les fonctions du πράκτωρ ξενικῶν", *CdE* 30, 1955, pp. 107–111.

Rabel 1933
Rabel, E., "Eine neue Vollmachtsurkunde", *Aegyptus* 13, 1933, pp. 374–380.

Rabel 1937
Rabel, E., "Systasis", *AHDO* 1, 1937, pp. 213–237.

Rabinowitz 1957–1958
Rabinowitz, J., "Miscellanea Papyrologica", *JJP* 11–12, 1957–1958, pp. 167–183.

Raschke 1974
Raschke, M.G., "The office of the *agoranomos* in Ptolemaic and Roman Egypt", in E. Kiessling, H.A. Rupprecht (eds.), *Akten des XIII. Internationalen Papyrologenkongresses, Marburg/Lahn, 2–6 August 1971*, MBPF 66, Munich, 1974, pp. 349–356.

Rathbone 1996
Rathbone, D.W., "Towards a Historical Topography of the Fayum", in D.M. Bailey (ed.), *Archaeological Research in Roman Egypt. The Proceedings of the Seventeenth Classical Colloquium of the Department of Greek and Roman Antiquities, British Museum*, JRA-Suppl. 19, Ann Arbor (Mich.), 1996, pp. 50–56.

Ratzan 2011
Ratzan, D.M., "Contract Norms and Contract Enforcement in Graeco-Roman Egypt", PhD Thesis, Columbia University, 2011.

Reiter 2002
Reiter, F., "P.Osl. inv. 1470 und die Webersteuer für Minderjährige in Oxyrhynchos", *APF* 48, 2002, pp. 128–131.

Rupprecht 1971
Rupprecht, H.-A., *Studien zur Quittung im Recht der graeco-ägyptischen Papyri*, MBPF 57, Munich, 1971.

Rupprecht 1997
Rupprecht, H.-A., "Zwangsvollstreckung und dingliche Sicherheiten in den Papyri der ptolemäischen und römischen Zeit", in G. Thür, J. Vélissaropoulos-Karakostas (eds.), *Symposion 1995. Vorträge zur griechischen und hellenistischen Rechtsgeschichte (Korfu, 1.–5. September 1995)*, AGR 11, Cologne, 1997, pp. 291–302.

Rupprecht/Kruse 2010
H.-A. Rupprecht, "Die Systasis - eine besondere Gestaltung in der Praxis der Papyri" and T. Kruse, "Antwort auf den Vortrag von H.-A. Rupprecht: 'Die Systasis - eine besondere Gestaltung in der Praxis der Papyri",' in: G. Thür (ed.) *Symposion 2009. Vorträge zur griechischen und hellenistischen Rechtsgeschichte*, AGR 21, Vienna, 2010, pp. 383–395, 397–404.

Rupprecht 2014
Rupprecht, H.-A., "Real Security", in J. Keenan, J. Manning, U. Yiftach-Firanko (eds.), *Law and Legal Practice in Egypt from Alexander to the Arab Conquest: A Selection of Papyrological Sources in Translation, with Introductions and Commentary*, Cambridge, 2014, pp. 249–275.

Russo 1999
Russo, S., *I gioielli nei papiri di età greco-romana*, Florence, 1999.

Scheidel 1996a
Scheidel, W., "Digit Preference in Age Records from Roman Egypt", in W. Scheidel, *Measuring Sex, Age and Death in the Roman Empire: Explorations in Ancient Demography*, JR-Suppl. 21, Ann Arbor (Mich.), 1996, pp. 53–91.

Scheidel 1996b
Scheidel, W., "What's in an Age? A Comparative View of Bias in the Census Returns of Roman Egypt", *BASP* 33, 1996, pp. 25–59.

Scherer 1942
Scherer, J., "Le Papyrus Fouad Ier, inv. 211", *BIFAO* 41, 1942, pp. 43–73.

Schmitz 1964
Schmitz, W., *He pistis in den Papyri*, Köln, 1964.

Schwarz 1937
Schwarz, A.B., "Sicherungsübereignung und Zwangsvollstreckung in den Papyri", *Aegyptus* 17, 1937, pp. 264–282.

Schwartz 1946
Schwartz, J., "Papyrus homériques", *BIFAO* 46, 1946, pp. 29–71.

Sijpesteijn 1996
Sijpesteijn, P.J., "Marriage Agreement with Property Division to Take Effect after Death and Other Documents", *ZPE* 111, 1996, pp. 163–170.

Sijpesteijn, Worp 1995
Sijpesteijn, P.J., Worp, K.A., "Ein Hausverkauf aus Soknopaiu Nesos (P. Lond. inv. 1976)", in R. Feenstra et al. (eds.), *Collatio iuris Romani. Études dédiées à Hans Ankum à l'occasion de son 65e anniversaire*, Amsterdam, 1995, pp. 512–532.

Solazzi 1924
Solazzi, S., "Le facoltá del procurator bonorum nel diritto romano-ellenico", *Aegyptus* 5, 1924, pp. 1–19.

Taubenschlag 1944 (ed. 1955)
Taubenschlag, R., *The Law of Greco-Roman Egypt in the Light of the Papyri, 332 B.C.–A.D. 640*, Warsaw, 1955 (2nd ed.).

Turner 2007
Turner, E.G., "Roman Oxyrhynchos", in A.K. Bowman et al. (eds.), *Oxyrhynchos: A City and Its Texts*, London, 2007, pp. 141–154.

Vandorpe 1991
Vandorpe, K., "Les villages des Ibis dans la toponymie tardive", *Enchoria* 18, 1991, pp. 115–122.

Verreth 2013
Verreth, H., *A Survey of Toponyms in Egypt in the Graeco-Roman Period*, TOP 2, 2013.

Wallace 1938
Wallace, S.L., *Taxation in Roman Egypt from Augustus to Diocletian*, Princeton University Studies in Papyrology 2, Princeton, 1938.

Wenger 1906
Wenger, L., *Die Stellvertretung im Recht der Papyri*, Leipzig, 1906.

Whitehorne 2006
Whitehorne, J., *Strategi and Royal Scribes of Roman Egypt*, PapFlor 37, Florence, 2006 (2nd ed.).

Wieacker 1931
Wieacker, F., "Εὐδόκησις und Kauf mit fremdem Geld", *ZSSR* 51, 1931, pp. 408–417.

Wilcken 1908
Wilcken, U., "Der ägyptische Konvent", *APF* 4, 1908, pp. 366–422.

Wilcken 1909
Wilcken, U., "Ehepatronae im römischen Kaiserhaus", *ZSSR* 30, 1909, pp. 504–507.

von Woess 1924
Woess, F. von, *Untersuchungen über das Urkundenwesen und den Publizitätsschutz im römischen Ägypten*, MBPF 6, Munich, 1924.

Wolff 1939
Wolff, H.J., Written and Unwritten Marriages in Hellenistic and Postclassical Roman Law, Philological Monographs publ. by the American Philological Association 9, Haverford, 1939.

Wolff 1941
Wolff, H.J., "The Praxis-Provision in Papyrus Contracts", *TAPA* 72, 1941, pp. 418–438.

Wolff 19780
Wolff, H.J., *Das Recht der griechischen Papyri Ägyptens in der Zeit der Ptolemäer und des Prinzipats* II: *Organisation und Kontrolle des privaten Rechtsverkehrs*, HAW 10.5, Munich, 1978.

Wolff 2002
Wolff, H.J., *Das Recht der griechischen Papyri Ägyptens in der Zeit der Ptolemäer und des Prinzipats I: Bedingungen und Triebkräfte der Rechtsentwicklung* (ed. H.-A. Rupprecht), HAW 10.5, Munich, 2002.

Yiftach-Firanko 2003
Yiftach-Firanko, U., *Marriage and Marital Arrangements: A History of the Greek Marriage Document in Egypt, 4th Century BCE – 4th Century CE*, MBPF 93, Munich, 2003.

Indexes

I. ROMAN EMPERORS AND THE IMPERIAL HOUSE

II. CHRONOLOGY

REGNAL YEARS

Antoninus Pius

Marcus Aurelius and Commodus

Caracalla and Geta

MONTHS

III. PERSONAL NAMES

The following abbreviations are used: **b.** = brother of; **d.** = daughter of; **f.** = father of; **gd.** = granddaughter of; **gf.** = grandfather of; **gs.** = grandson of; **h.** = husband of; **m.** = mother of, his mother being; **s.** = son of; **sis.** = sister of; **w.** = wife of.

IV. GEOGRAPHICAL AND TOPOGRAPHICAL NAMES

V. TRIBES AND DEMES

VI. TITLES AND FUNCTIONS

VII. MEASURES AND COINS

VIII. GENERAL

DIFFUSION
Ventes directes et par correspondance

Au Caire
à l'Ifao,
37 rue al-Cheikh Ali Youssef (Mounira)
[B.P. Qasr al-ᶜAyni 11562]
11441 Le Caire, Égypte
Section Diffusion Vente

Tél.: (+20 2) 27 90 02 55
https://www.ifao.egnet.net

mél: diffusion@ifao.egnet.net

En France
Vente en librairies

***Diffusion* AFPU-D**
C/O Université de Lille
3 rue du Barreau
BP 60149 - 59653 Villeneuve-d'Ascq Cedex
Tél. +33 (0)3 20 41 66 95

***Distribution* DILISCO**
Zone artisanale Les Conduits
Rue du Limousin
BP 25 - 23220 Cheniers
Tél. +33 (0)5 55 51 80 00

Ministère de l'Enseignement supérieur et de la Recherche, Paris
Publication de l'Institut français d'archéologie orientale
Achevé d'imprimer sur les presses de l'Ifao, 37 rue al-Cheikh Ali Youssef au Caire, en février 2024
Dépôt légal: 1er semestre 2024; N° éditeur: 7247